"Sam Storms has blessed me so many times through his life and ministry, but the honesty and hope of this book moved me in a special way. We all need help to keep going when life brings suffering, and Sam teaches us how: look to the steadfast love of the Lord. Sam shows us how to take refuge in God's love even when we cannot understand his ways (which will surely happen to us all). This richly biblical series of meditations will be edifying to everyone who reads it and will bring special comfort and strength to those who are struggling with doubts or spiritual dryness."

Gavin Ortlund, President, Truth Unites; Theologian-in-Residence, Immanuel Church, Nashville, Tennessee

"When the Creator of the universal calls himself 'I AM,' he reminds us that he is in control, through the good times and the bad. Those words also remind us that God loves us—unconditionally, passionately, consistently. He loves us when a child dies, when a cancer diagnosis is made, when a marriage crumbles, and when death arrives. We may not know why we experience these trials, but we can know with absolute assurance that God's love for us is steadfast, never changing, always present. Drink in the pages of this book and let Sam Storms remind you that God is love—and that he will always love you."

Janet Parshall, nationally syndicated talk show host

"This new book by veteran Bible teacher Sam Storms is a spiritually refreshing, joy-inspiring, pastorally wise study of one of the most important concepts in the Bible: God's steadfast love. Readers of this book will find themselves overwhelmed by a deeper, fuller awareness of God's loving presence."

Wayne Grudem, Distinguished Research Professor Emeritus of Theology and Biblical Studies, Phoenix Seminary

"For years, long after earning a PhD in theology, my greatest theological struggle has been an almost subconscious doubt of God's love for me. I knew this truth in my head, of course, but struggled to grasp the reality with my heart. I am thankful for Storms's scripturally faithful and pastorally insightful treatment of this incredible subject. I only wish I'd read it sooner! Someone once said that the gospel is like a well: the best water is found by going deeper. We simply cannot steep ourselves in the gospel of God's love enough. Enjoy this book."

J. D. Greear, author, *Gospel: Recovering the Power that Made Christianity Revolutionary* and *12 Truths and a Lie: Answers to Life's Biggest Questions*

The Steadfast Love of the Lord

The Steadfast Love of the Lord

Experiencing the Life-Changing Power
of God's Unchanging Affection

Sam Storms

Foreword by Dane Ortlund

:: CROSSWAY®

WHEATON, ILLINOIS

Library of Congress Cataloging-in-Publication Data

Names: Storms, C. Samuel, 1951– author.
Title: The steadfast love of the Lord : experiencing the life-changing power of God's unchanging affection / Sam Storms.
Description: Wheaton, Illinois : Crossway, 2025. | Includes bibliographical references and index.
Identifiers: LCCN 2024000068 (print) | LCCN 2024000069 (ebook) | ISBN 9781433593871 (trade paperback) | ISBN 9781433593888 (pdf) | ISBN 9781433593895 (epub)
Subjects: LCSH: God (Christianity)—Love. | Love—Religious aspects—Christianity. | Holy Spirit.
Classification: LCC BT140 .S787 2025 (print) | LCC BT140 (ebook) | DDC 231/.6—dc23/eng/20240621
LC record available at https://lccn.loc.gov/2024000068
LC ebook record available at https://lccn.loc.gov/2024000069

Contents

Foreword

THE WONDROUS SECRET soaking this anguish-laden universe is a divine love that befriends and embraces and even substitutes for the undeserving. Sam Storms knows this. And in *The Steadfast Love of the Lord*, he takes us into the wonders of that love as only he can.

I say "as only he can" because Sam is a rare constellation of at least four giftings. And in God's mercy Sam has proven himself over the years to be experienced and faithful—and therefore trusted—in each one.

First, Sam is an exegete. He loves the Bible, and he handles it well. Coming upon biblical texts in this book is like coming upon lush greenery in a jungle, confronting us at each step. Sam was trained well early on in the original languages and in how to handle God's word, and that facility with the text has deepened rather than plateaued over his many years of pastoring and teaching. Sam knows that without a Bible he would have nothing to say. And he operates accordingly.

Second, Sam is a theologian. He thinks deeply and wisely and biblically about God. He thinks with balance and nuance when called for but also with boldness and courage when called for. He is well aware of the past generations of church leaders who have gone before us, and therefore is not drawn to passing theological fads. He does theology in the context of the local church. He sings and celebrates his theology, rather than only dissect and analyze. He is everything a Christian theologian should be.

Third, Sam is a pastor. A shepherd. He writes not to build himself up but to build the flock up. And so he aims not only at our minds but at our hearts through our minds, for he's after the soul. That's what animates every faithful shepherd. The obvious goal of this book, consistent with Sam's whole life, is to address the real-life agitations of soul that each one of us is negotiating every hour of every day. Even in seasons of life serving as a professor, Sam has given himself with all his heart to the local church.

Fourth, Sam is a lover. He is a man of burning heart and bright energies and strong affections. He does not write and teach with flat emotional monotony. If he did, he would betray the very subject matter of this book. God's love for his own is uproarious, sparkling with the explosive delight of which the most profound human affections are a faint mirage. The author of *The Steadfast Love of the Lord* lives his life, and writes this book, acutely mindful of this love. Such a man deserves our attention when he sits down to write of this grand theme.

I can't resist adding a fifth point that made the reading of this manuscript a joy—he's a friend. I commend this book to you accordingly. Throughout the spring of 2001, as a twenty-two-year-old, I sat on the second floor of Jenks Hall at Wheaton College as Dr. Storms walked us through the basic tenets of evangelical systematic theology. But he not only taught me; he befriended me, through lunches and prayer times. And he has been a friend and encourager ever since.

What startled me wonderfully in that 2001 Wheaton class was not so much the content of what was taught but the tone with which that content about God was handled—the tone of celebration, the reverence in handling God's very word, the wonder at God's beauty, the humility at being delivered by grace and grace alone, the longing for every student to experience God's endless wonders as we sat with Bible open. This is the very tone you will find in this book.

Dane Ortlund

SENIOR PASTOR,

NAPERVILLE PRESBYTERIAN CHURCH;

AUTHOR, *GENTLE AND LOWLY*

Introduction

Doubting the Love of God

I HAVE A CONFESSION TO MAKE, and it needs to happen before you read another word of this book. Rarely in my Christian life have I struggled with doubt. My faith has almost always been rock-solid and robust. Sure, there were times when I was confused by things I read in Scripture, times when I shook my head in measured disbelief. But I don't believe I ever seriously wavered in my confidence that God is both good and loving.

Then a 7.8 earthquake struck southeastern Turkey in the spring of 2023. You may remember that day, as word began to spread of several thousand who had died in the rubble of countless buildings and homes that crumbled like they were made of toothpicks. At first, the report was that 6,000 had perished. Later that same day, the number grew to 15,000. The next day, we were told that it was over 30,000 and would probably increase as the rescue efforts escalated. The last time I checked the death toll had risen to over 59,000.

Joseph Stalin, Russian dictator who succeeded Vladimir Lenin in the aftermath of the October Revolution, is reported to have said,

"One death is a tragedy, a million deaths a statistic."[1] How coldly brutal and uncaring that is. But I understand the sentiment. As the number of those who died in Turkey and Syria continued to climb each day, I began to lose sight that each number represented a human being, several thousand of whom were under the age of five. We weep over one death, but a fog of indifference clouds our souls when the number is so great that the people who died become little more than an unidentifiable mass.

The news broke that one woman gave birth beneath the pile of heavy slabs of concrete under which she was buried. Her newborn infant survived, but she did not. That was hard enough for me to swallow. Then I watched on the news as another grieving mother rocked her lifeless two-month-old baby boy in her arms. I couldn't hold back the tears and, well, the anger too. "God, where are you? Where were you when this happened? I know your power is without limit and that you could have as easily put a stop to the earthquake with as little effort as Jesus exerted when he silenced the wind and waves on the Sea of Galilee. So why did you let this happen?"

I knew I was drawing close to crossing a line in my complaint to the Lord. Oh, how very close I came to accusing him of sin, of failing to act consistently with what he says about himself in Scripture, of not caring about the depths of pain and anguish so many people had experienced.

It was then that I began to struggle with the reality of God's love. Honestly, I'm still struggling. You may think it odd that I would write a book extolling the steadfast love of God at the same time I'm wrestling with doubts about it in my heart. But I'm not being duplicitous. I have no desire to be a hypocrite. I simply realized

---

1   "Joseph Stalin, 1879–1953," in *Oxford Essential Quotations*, ed. Susan Ratcliffe (Oxford: Oxford University Press, 2016), https://www.oxfordreference.com/.

that the only way I was going to press through this dark season in my soul was to bathe it in the repeated theme of Scripture that "the steadfast love of the Lord never ceases" (Lam. 3:22).

I wish I could say that my heart is now at perfect peace when contemplating the truth of God's steadfast love, but alas, it is not. However, I am sufficiently calm and convinced that what the Bible says about God is true and so I can proceed with writing this short book. In fact, the more I thought and prayed about it, the more I came to the same conclusion of the disciples in John 6 when the difficult words of Jesus had driven away so many of his professed followers. "Do you want to go away as well?" Jesus asked them (John 6:67). Peter spoke for all of them (and for me too) when he replied, "Lord, to whom shall we go? You have the words of eternal life" (John 6:68).

Where else can I turn if not to the truth of the steadfast, never-ending, always-faithful love of God? Even if I can't account for earthquakes in Turkey or tornadoes in my home state of Oklahoma or widespread famine in Sudan, what options do I have? What options do you have? If God's love isn't real and steady and ultimately steadfast, what hope do any of us have? To what philosophy of life will we turn? To the words of what sage will we listen?

As I began writing this book, I received an email from a man in my church here in Oklahoma City. He had a question for me, one that I struggled to answer:

Sam,

I have a good friend whose oldest son committed suicide a few days ago. I was wondering if you could share a few high-level insights/wisdom from your experience with walking with someone going through this. So far, the little I've been able to talk

with my friend I've just said I'm sorry and asked what I can do.
Some things I've thought about are:
What kind of answer would you give to a question of why God
would allow something like this?
How is God good if this happens?
How does this become redeemed for good?
How is this God's love for me, my family, and my dead son?
Etc . . .
Again, he hasn't asked any of these questions, but, when ap-
propriate, I want to point him to the scripture and Jesus. My
primary answer in my mind is, "I don't know, and I'm sorry this
happened." Any thoughts you'd have I'd welcome.[2]

How would you have answered an email like this? I certainly
didn't want to respond with a series of spiritual platitudes that
sound insightful but ultimately accomplish little. I don't know if
this helped, but this is what I wrote back to him:

The last thing that someone who's experienced this sort of tragedy
wants to hear is a theological explanation of why it happened.
Even if you could give him one, it wouldn't diminish the pain or
sense of loss he feels. Situations like this remind me of Job. He
lost all his children and possessions and his "friends" labored to
give him an explanation why it happened. This only aggravated
his condition. When these things happen, the best thing to do
is to keep your mouth shut and sit and weep with your friend.
You are right when you say "I don't know" is the best response.
We don't know why these things happen and God doesn't tell

2 This quotation is from the author's personal experience.

us. What he tells us is that he is good and will never leave or forsake us. That may not help much, but anything else or more will only sound flippant and uncaring to him.

I'm not suggesting we are always in the wrong for trying to decipher God's ways and to make sense of what strikes us as senseless. But in some instances, such as this man's loss of his son, I am more inclined to put my hand over my mouth and simply reflect on Paul's words in Romans 11:33–36:

> Oh, the depth of the riches and wisdom and knowledge of God! How unsearchable are his judgments and how inscrutable his ways! For who has known the mind of the Lord, or who has been his counselor? Or who has given a gift to him that he might be repaid? For from him and through him and to him are all things. To him be glory forever. Amen.

I know that sounds like a cop-out. In fact, it almost comes across as one of those spiritual platitudes that I earlier said I would never espouse. But let's be honest. What other options are there? To theologize this man's loss of his son to suicide, as if any of us is capable of accounting for why God performs or permits such tragedies to occur, sounds trivial to the hurting heart. Indescribably painful too. I could envision this father saying in response, "My son's life is worth more than a doctrinal declaration. How can you so casually write off his tragic and premature death with your supposed insight into the mysteries of the universe?"

So where does that leave us? If it's OK with you, I'm going to stick with the apostle Paul. Do you really believe there are other viable options? I don't. I'm left clinging in my feeble, oh-so-very-tenuous faith to the unsearchable judgments and inscrutable ways of God. I simply don't know where or to whom I can turn, other than to say that "all things"—yes, even the incomprehensibly devastating death of one's child—are "from" God and exist "through" God and ultimately will be seen as bringing glory and honor "to" God.

After more than a half century in Christian ministry, after hearing and personally witnessing countless instances of this sort of disastrous news, I remain a believer in the steadfast love of God. That doesn't mean I can easily explain why this man's son took his own life or why God allowed the earthquake in Turkey, the slaughter of millions by Stalin, the deaths incurred during COVID-19, or the sexual abuse of precious young children all around our country. I can't. And neither can you. But if God's love is no more than a pipe dream, a cloud without rain, a promise with no hope of fulfillment, then we are of all people most to be pitied (1 Cor. 15:19).

But don't misunderstand me. I'm not saying that the only or even primary reason I remain confident of the truth of God's love is that I have no other options, far less because it provides me with the psychological boost I need to get out of bed each day. I believe it and am happy to write about it for at least three reasons.

First, I believe it because the Holy Spirit has strengthened my inner being with divine power to "comprehend with all the saints what is the breadth and length and height and depth, and to know the love of Christ that surpasses knowledge" (Eph. 3:18–19). There is indelibly imprinted in the innermost recesses of my soul the unshakeable conviction that God is love. I didn't put it there. The Holy Spirit did.

More than that, the Holy Spirit has deeply embedded in my soul an unassailable assurance that what Scripture says about God's love is true. He has opened the eyes of my heart and enlightened my feeble mind to rest confidently in the truth of the inspired text that tells me repeatedly that God's love is genuine and steadfast.

Finally, I believe in God's steadfast love because of the way it was demonstrated in the gift from God the Father of God the Son to die for me on the cross as expressed in passages like Romans 5:6–11 and 8:32. I'll have more to say later about these passages, but let it be known now that the only explanation for the cross of Christ is the steadfast love of God for his own. The apostle John said it best and most succinctly: "In this the love of God was made manifest among us, that God sent his only Son into the world, so that we might live through him. In this is love, not that we loved God but that he loved us and sent his Son to be the propitiation for our sins" (1 John 4:9–10).

Yes, I'll continue to grapple in my heart with the multitude of natural disasters that I wake up to almost every day. And I will not offer trite explanations for why humans continue to commit horrid acts of perversion and evil against each other. Even if I could, no one, not even me, would be convinced by them. But I cannot, I will not, allow my intellectual shortcomings to account for the problem of evil to blind me to the bright light of the everlasting, unchanging, soul-saving, steadfast love of God.

1

Love Is Love. Or Is It?

IT ONLY MAKES SENSE that before we dive into an exploration of the steadfast love of God that we define love itself. You may think that's a no-brainer, but the distortions of love in our world today have made this a somewhat arduous task.

You may remember when news broke that contemporary Christian music icon Amy Grant decided to host a so-called same-sex wedding on her property. In response to the pushback she received, this is what she said: "I never chase any of those rabbits down the rabbit hole. I love my family, I love those brides. They're wonderful, our family is better, and you should be able to be who you are with your family, and be loved by them."[1]

She previously told the *Washington Post* how she justified in her mind the same-sex wedding, saying that she was just loving them like Jesus would: "Jesus, you just narrowed it down to two things: love God and love each other'. . . I mean, hey—that's pretty simple."[2] In case you

---

1   Brenton Blanchet and Topher Gauk-Roger, "Amy Grant on Homophobic Criticism Over Niece's Same-Sex Wedding: 'I Love Those Brides,'" *People*, January 16, 2023, https://people.com/.
2   Blanchet and Gauk-Roger, "Amy Grant on Homophobic Criticism."

haven't figured it out by now, her definition of "love" affirms whatever lifestyle choices a person prefers as morally legitimate. On this view, it is hateful or bigoted to suggest that such a marriage is sinful, immoral, and potentially exposes an individual to eternal damnation.

I've always appreciated Grant, her professed commitment to Christ, and, yes, her music as well. My purpose in citing this incident isn't to cast aspersions on her character but simply to highlight how the world and its mindset has infected the Christian community with its distorted and profoundly unbiblical understanding of what constitutes love.

Most of us have at some point felt or experienced what we believed was love. For some of you, it was that tingling sensation in your abdomen or perhaps a shiver down your spine when you first came into contact with that special someone. For others, it was the thrill of being in the presence of a person who had captivated your affections and made you feel special and highly valued. Some would insist that love has nothing to do with feelings at all but is entirely a volitional choice to bless another or to sacrifice greatly for their welfare. These are expressions of love in horizontal relationships between men and women. But what do the biblical authors mean when they speak of God's steadfast love for sinners like you and me? Sadly, there is considerable confusion today when it comes to nailing down a definition of love.

Defining Love

These days I regularly see a new slogan emblazoned on T-shirts, the bumper stickers of cars, placards held high at rallies, and even the back of the football helmets of NFL players: "Love is love!"

My first reaction, as you might guess, is to ask a question of any person promoting this philosophy, "Please, define 'love.'" The answer in return would probably be something along the lines of, "I just did. I said, 'love is love.'" This answer is obviously circular, and any attempt to communicate meaningfully with a person who takes this approach is probably doomed from the outset.

So what do people mean when they say that "Love is love"? Unless I'm mistaken, I think they mean what Amy Grant meant— that love is always accepting, never critical, entirely inclusive, and altogether affirming of the moral legitimacy of anything a person believes and however they choose to behave. To push back and argue that certain beliefs are false is not loving. It is hateful. To suggest that a particular lifestyle is morally perverse is not loving. It is bigoted. To employ any language that does not affirm the truth or legitimacy of something another person believes or does is an expression of intolerance and will probably subject you to being cancelled in some way.

It's important to observe the transformation of a crucial term in our world today: tolerance. Tolerance once meant granting a person the freedom to believe whatever they want and behave however they choose as long as neither their belief nor behavior was detrimental to another person or society at large. So there was always a limit to tolerance, a certain boundary beyond which one could not go. But no longer.

Tolerance today means not only that you don't interfere with or prohibit someone from believing a certain idea or doctrine that differs from your own but also that you vigorously affirm that their belief is just as true and legitimate as yours. Tolerance has effectively prohibited any use of the words "wrong," "misguided," "false," and "immoral." Of course, the great irony in this is that saying, in the name of tolerance, that it is "wrong" or "misguided" to claim that someone else's belief or behavior is "wrong" or "misguided" is, by their own definition, profoundly intolerant! But I won't linger on that point here.[3]

The best illustration of this is the furious debate in our society over the subject of homosexuality and transgenderism. In Romans 12:9 Paul exhorts us to "let love be genuine," and in Romans 12:10 he commands us to "love one another with brotherly affection." But he also says in Romans 1 that some expressions of human sexuality are impure, dishonorable, contrary to nature, shameful, and deserving of eternal judgment. So how can one be loving and yet say such things about homosexual conduct?

I suspect that many people in our society, perhaps even most, would insist that it is impossible to consistently embrace both positions. As noted, they argue that to tell someone that his or her sexual behavior is dishonorable and shameful is not loving, and if we are to love someone, we must affirm their choices and never suggest that what they are doing is morally impure or wrong or sinful. This would appear to be the stance assumed by Grant.

I bring this to our attention yet again because of events in Finland that unfolded in 2022. The news was all over the internet regarding "a Christian politician from Finland who ha[d] been formally charged with three counts of hate speech against homosexuals and face[d] two years in prison if convicted."[4] According to one news outlet, Paivi Rasanen,

a member of the Finnish Parliament, has been under investigation since 2019 for social media posts questioning the Evangelical

---

3   For a fuller treatment of this subject, see D. A. Carson, *The Intolerance of Tolerance* (Grand Rapids, MI: Eerdmans, 2012).

4   Dale Hurd, "Finnish Lawmaker Faces Trial for Hate Speech After Quoting the Bible About Homosexuality," CBN, April 30, 2021, https://www2.cbn.com/.

Lutheran Church's official affiliation with the Helsinki LGBT Pride event. In her posts, Rasanen showed a photo of the Bible passage Romans 1:24–27, which condemns homosexuality as a sin. She is also charged for a pamphlet she wrote in 2004 entitled "Male and female He created them: Homosexual relationships challenge the Christian concept of humanity," in which she said that God designed marriage for one man and one woman. And she's accused of hate speech for comments she made about homosexuality on a Christian TV program in Finland.[5]

Rasanen courageously stood by her convictions and refused to apologize for her writings or for the writings of the apostle Paul. As I write this chapter, I learned that though the initial charges against her were dropped, they had recently been revived. I'm sure that by the time of this book's publication a final verdict will have been rendered.

I contend that what Rasanen said and wrote is a profound expression of love and compassion, and that for her *not* to have spoken in such terms would have been an equally profound expression of hate and utter disregard for the temporal and eternal welfare of practicing homosexuals. Let me say it clearly: to tell someone who is living in unrepentant homosexuality that his or her behavior is dishonorable, morally wrong, and puts their soul in jeopardy of eternal damnation is the most loving thing you could possibly say to them. I know that this runs counter to our society's perspective today, but I don't regard the world or its opinions as authoritative. Only God's written word is authoritative. Only Scripture is decisive in telling me what is right and wrong and what the eternal consequences of both are.

5   Hurd, "Finnish Lawmaker Faces Trial for Hate Speech."

And that leads me to what may well be the most important thing I can say regarding this issue—the entire debate and the division that it creates boils down to a question of one's ultimate moral authority. You have a choice to make, and you have only two options: either you acknowledge and submit to the authoritative statements of the Bible or you acknowledge and submit to the passions, feelings, and opinions of your own soul. Either God defines your identity in his word or you define it according to your good pleasure. Either God decides what is true, good, false, and evil or you do. Either you believe that personal identity is self-chosen, self-constructed, based on one's personal preferences and desires or you believe that it is God-given and defined by him in Scripture. Either the God of the Bible is your God or your own autonomous self is your god.

So when the Bible says that sexual relations between two people of the same gender is sinful, either you embrace that as morally definitive because the Bible is authoritative or you reject it because your own soul is authoritative. What is it going to be—self or Scripture? Who or what is your final authority? Once that is decided, the rest of what lies before us is quite simple. Once that is decided, the meaning of true and genuine love is quite simple.

Yet, if we choose God's way, we face another type of obstacle in addressing this issue—how we will be treated by the world. Simply stated, to believe what the Bible says on this subject is to open yourself to the charge of homophobia. Although that word literally means "a fear of homosexuality," it is used today as part of a strategy of intimidation to silence Christians and squash dissent from the mainstream view. Christians will also be charged with being intolerant and bigoted. Others will accuse us of being opposed to diversity and guilty of discrimination. Some will even claim that by speaking critically of homosexual behavior, we incite violence against people who are attracted to someone of the same sex. Thus, we will be mocked and ridiculed for holding to what is considered an outmoded, outdated, primitive understanding of human sexuality. Moreover, embracing the authority of God on this issue may well put us in legal jeopardy, be that in the form of criminal charges (as in Finland), a monetary fine, or getting cancelled.

So what are we to do? The answer, at least to me, is obvious. We humbly search out Scripture to determine what it says about human sexual behavior and we then embrace it and submit to it, no matter the social or personal cost that may entail. "But Sam," some will say, "why is it important for us to address this topic? Why can't we just skip over Romans 1 and other biblical texts and move on to more important matters?"

The answer is obvious. We must address this issue because (1) the Bible does! Our primary commitment is to truth, and this must take precedence over all other considerations; (2) we cannot fully follow Christ if our sexuality is out of step with God's design; (3) the urgency of our specific time and place in history demands that we speak out; and (4) unrepentant homosexual conduct puts a person's soul in jeopardy of eternal damnation.

Now, let me say three more things about how we are to love other people. First, we must denounce any tendency by anyone to dehumanize homosexuals or to suggest that they are not made in the image of God. People who struggle with same-sex attraction are just as human as you and deserve to be treated with as much dignity as you. Second, our attitude toward those who identify as homosexual or who struggle with same-sex attraction must be one of loving concern, compassion, and a desire to help. Third, we should pray that what we say about homosexuality, together with the way that we all interact with and respond to people who struggle in this regard, will make them want to stay in our churches, not run away. We must labor to speak and act in such a way that all people, regardless of their sexual conduct, will find in us a loving, helping, and compassionate church. Simply put, the church of Jesus Christ should be a place where those who experience same-sex attraction can find the power of the Holy Spirit to overcome their sinful desires and change or, if not, can find the strength, courage, help, and love from us to live a joyful and triumphant life of celibacy.

So is love "love"? As we've seen, it all depends on how you define "love." My definition, the Bible's definition, is that "love" is acting and speaking in such a way that the object of one's affection is blessed in this life and in the age to come. It is never loving to speak or act in such a way that a person is encouraged to continue to believe or behave in a manner that, according to Scripture, puts their soul in jeopardy of eternal damnation (1 Cor. 6:9–11; Gal. 5:19–21; Eph. 5:5–6). To truly love a person you must say and do all that you can to direct them to beliefs and behaviors that align with their eternal destiny in the presence of God in the new heaven and new earth. That is love.

God's Love for Us

So what about God's love? To speak of our love for other men and women is one thing. But this book is concerned with God's love for us. To put it as simply as possible, to say that God loves us means that he is passionately committed to providing us with whatever is needed so that we might flourish now and in eternity. It means he is devoted to satisfying our souls with the one thing that will thoroughly captivate our hearts now and forevermore. And that one thing is himself! This certainly calls for some explanation. And in order to make sense of it all I need to demonstrate the connection between what is known as Christian hedonism and the love of God for sinners like you and me.

The problem we face is that Scripture presents to us two undeniable truths that on the surface appear to be mutually exclusive. One would think that it simply isn't possible to hold both simultaneously. The first and most obvious truth of Scripture is that God has created the universe, which includes us, in order that he might be glorified. God's preeminent passion is to draw attention to himself and to display the majestic beauty of his own being. To be perfectly blunt about it, God's chief end in all he does is himself. But if God is preeminently for himself, how can he be for me and you? If his first and greatest love is for himself, how can he love us at all?

God's love for himself strikes us at first glance to be profoundly selfish and utterly at odds with what Scripture says about his love for us. It appears to rule out any possibility that he can sincerely love people in a way that is real and heartfelt. But the apparent contradiction is only a mirage.

To understand this, let's return to our fundamental definition of love. If God is to truly love us, he must be altogether consumed to provide us with the greatest joy, gladness, and satisfaction of soul that is possible for a human to experience. So how might he do that? The answer is obvious, once you've given it some thought. If God is to fill our hearts and minds with the greatest degree of delight and joy, he would have to give us the most delightful and joyful person in the universe. And who might that be? God, of course!

Christian Hedonism and the Steadfast Love of God

There was a time when I thought my happiness and God's glory were mutually exclusive.[6] I had to choose between one or the other;

---

6   Portions of this section are taken from Sam Storms, "Christian Hedonism: Piper and Edwards on the Pursuit of Joy in God," in *For the Fame of God's Name: Essays in Honor of John Piper*, ed. Sam Storms and Justin Taylor (Wheaton, IL: Crossway, 2010). Used by permission.

embracing them both struck me as out of the question. Worse still, enjoying God sounded a bit too lighthearted, almost casual, perhaps even flippant, and I knew that Christianity was serious business.

Then I read Jonathan Edwards (1703–1758) and his contemporary disciple (and now my longtime friend) John Piper. These two men helped me to see that God's glory and my gladness were not antithetical. They helped me see that at the core of Scripture is the truth that my heart's passion for pleasure (which is God-given, not the result of sin) and God's passion for praise converge in a way that makes sense of all human existence. There is one statement from Edwards that is one of the most significant and life-changing utterances I've ever read. He writes,

> Now what is glorifying God, but a rejoicing at that glory he has displayed? An understanding of the perfections of God, merely, cannot be the end of the creation; for he had as good not understand it, as see it and not be at all moved with joy at the sight. Neither can the highest end of creation be the declaring God's glory to others; for the declaring God's glory is good for nothing otherwise than to raise joy in ourselves and others at what is declared.[7]

Edwards's point is that passionate and joyful admiration of God—not merely acknowledgement and intellectual apprehension—is the aim of our existence. If God is to be supremely glorified in us, we must be supremely glad in him and in what he has done for us in Jesus. Enjoying God is not a secondary, tangential endeavor. It is central to everything we do, especially worship. We

---

7   Jonathan Edwards, *The Miscellanies*, in *The Works of Jonathan Edwards*, vol. 13, ed. Thomas A. Schafer (New Haven, CT: Yale University Press, 1994), 200.

do not do other things hoping that joy in God will emerge as a by-product. Our reason for pursuing God and obeying him is to gain the joy that is found in him alone. Ultimately, to worship him for any reason other than the joy that is found in him is sinful.

Some object to Christian hedonism because of their aversion to the notion that we are to seek our joyful satisfaction in God without limitations or boundaries. I was greatly helped in overcoming my own struggle with this by something Edwards said in his sermon on the Song of Solomon 5:1. Here is Edwards's translation of the text: "Eat, O friends; drink, yea, drink abundantly, O beloved."[8] Although most today believe that the Song of Solomon addresses the love relationship between husband and wife, Edwards stood in the tradition that dominated church history for its first 1,800 years by arguing that this book was an allegory or poetic portrayal of the love relationship between Christ and the church or believer. His sermon on this text, preached in 1729, was titled "Spiritual Appetites Need No Bounds."

Edwards's main point is that when it comes to satisfying our souls with the spiritual delights and joys found in Christ, there are no excesses, no boundaries, no limitations. Edwards refers to these affections and desires as holy "inclinations." He continues,

> Persons neither need nor ought to keep those inclinations and desires from increasing to any degree whatsoever, and there cannot be a too frequent or too powerful exercise of them. . . . By not setting any bounds to those appetites, is meant not laying any restraint upon ourselves with respect to gratifying of them. Persons may indulge them as much as they please; they may

8 Kyle C. Strobel, Adriaan C. Neele, and Kenneth P. Minkema, eds., *Jonathan Edwards, Spiritual Writings* (New York: Paulist Press, 2019), 142.

give themselves their full swing. They may not only allow a very eager thirst and enlarged desire, but they may drink their fill; there is no excess. . . . They may drink, yea, swim in the rivers of spiritual pleasure.[9]

When Edwards turned to make application of this truth, he urged all "to promote spiritual appetites by laying yourself in the way of allurement."[10] What he meant by this is that we are responsible for taking advantage of every opportunity to position our souls in a way that will increase the potential and likelihood for us to be captivated and satisfied by the blessings offered in Christ. Again, he writes,

> We ought to take all opportunities to lay ourselves in the way of enticement with respect to our gracious inclinations. Thus you should be often with God in prayer, and then you will be in the way of having your heart drawn forth to him. We ought to be frequent in reading and constant in hearing the word. And particularly to this end, we ought carefully and with the utmost seriousness and consideration attend the sacrament of the Lord's Supper: this was appointed for this end, to draw forth the longings of our souls toward Jesus Christ.[11]

I can't envision any better news for the believer than this. God, because of his steadfast love, has prepared an exquisite banquet for us of the most glorious truths, promises, power, and blessings possible. So come and eat to the full! Come and drink and be satis-

9   Strobel, Neele, and Minkema, *Jonathan Edwards*, 145–46.
10 Strobel, Neele, and Minkema, *Jonathan Edwards*, 151.
11 Strobel, Neele, and Minkema, *Jonathan Edwards*, 151.

fied with all that God is for you in Jesus! Indulge yourself. There is no such thing as too much! Or, as Piper has said so often before, God is most glorified in us when we are most satisfied and filled with the joy of knowing him in Christ Jesus.[12] That is the essence of Christian hedonism.

The next step is a difficult one for some to take. It is one thing to say that God is most glorified in our glad-hearted delight in him. It is something else entirely to say our glad-hearted passion for God is exceeded only by God's glad-hearted passion for himself. If the chief end of man is to glorify God by enjoying him forever, the chief end of God is to glorify God and to enjoy himself forever!

I'm talking about the preeminent passion in God's heart, his greatest and singular delight. In what does God rejoice most? Or to put it bluntly, what is God's greatest love? I believe that the preeminent passion in God's heart is his own glory. God is at the center of his own affections. The supreme love of God's life is God. God is preeminently committed to the fame of his name. God is himself the end for which he created the world. Better still, God's immediate goal in all he does is his own glory. God relentlessly and unceasingly creates, rules, orders, directs, speaks, judges, saves, destroys, and delivers in order to make known who he is and to secure from the whole of the universe the praise, honor, and glory that he and he alone is ultimately and infinitely worthy of.

The question I most often hear in response to this is that if God loves himself preeminently, how can he love me at all? How can we say that God is for us and that he desires our happiness if he is primarily for himself and his own glory? I want to argue that it is precisely *because* God loves himself that he loves you. Here's how:

12   John Piper, *Desiring God: Meditations of a Christian Hedonist* (Colorado Springs: Multnomah Books, 2011), 17–28.

I assume you will agree that your greatest good consists of enjoying, delighting in, and being indescribably satisfied with the most excellent Being in the universe. That Being, of course, is God. Therefore, the most loving and kind thing that God can do for you is to devote all his energy and effort to elicit from your heart praise of himself. Why? Because praise is the consummation of your enjoyment. All enjoyment tends toward praise and adoration as its appointed end. In this way, God seeking his own glory and God seeking your good converge.

Listen again. Your greatest good is in the enjoyment of God. God's greatest glory is in being enjoyed. So God seeking his glory in your worship of him is the most loving thing he can do for you. Only by seeking his glory preeminently can God seek your good passionately. God working for your enjoyment of him (that's his love for you) and his glory in being enjoyed (that's his love for himself) are not properly separate.

To help you understand more clearly the nature of Christian hedonism and how it relates to God's steadfast love for his people, I direct your attention to something C. S. Lewis discovered and wrote about in an essay titled "A Word about Praising." It is found in his short volume *Reflections on the Psalms*.[13] Lewis helped me to recognize that the enjoyment of God is an essential feature of Christian worship. He roots this conclusion in the nature of praise itself: "I think we delight to praise what we enjoy because the praise not merely expresses but completes the enjoyment; it is its appointed consummation."[14] Lewis continued, "I had never noticed that all enjoyment spontaneously overflows into praise unless . . . shyness or the fear of boring others is deliberately brought in to check it . . .

---

13 C. S. Lewis, *Reflections on the Psalms* (San Diego: Harcourt Brace Jovanovich, 1958), 90–98.
14 Lewis, *Reflections on the Psalms*, 94.

Except where intolerably adverse circumstances interfere, praise almost seems to be inner health made audible."[15]

What Lewis is touching on here is how the steadfast love of God for sinners like you and me is ultimately made manifest. God desires our greatest good, which is undeniably our experience of himself. So if God is truly to love us, he must give us himself. But giving us himself is only the first step in the expression of his affection for sinners. He must work to elicit from our hearts rapturous praise and superlative delight because, as Lewis said, "all enjoyment spontaneously overflows into praise." That's the way God made us. We can't help but praise and rejoice in what we most enjoy. The enjoyment itself is stunted and hindered if it is never expressed in joyful celebration.

So, if I understand Lewis correctly, he's telling us that God's pursuit of my praise of him is not self-seeking but the epitome of self-giving, steadfast love! If my satisfaction in him is incomplete until expressed in praise of him for satisfying me with himself, then God's effort to elicit my worship (what Lewis before thought was inexcusable selfishness) is both the most loving thing he could possibly do for me and the most glorifying thing he could possibly do for himself, for my gladness in him (not his gifts but his intrinsic beauty) is his glory in me. This, then, is the essence and beauty of Christian hedonism and the nature of God's steadfast love for us.

---

15 Lewis, *Reflections on the Psalms*, 94.

2

How Long Will God's Love Last?

FOR QUITE A FEW of you reading this book, the word "steadfast" is perhaps the last word you would ever associate with love. Your experience may well be that people loudly profess their love for you and promise that they will never leave you, betray you, or love another the way they love you but then leave. You reached out for them in a time of darkness or desperation and discovered you were grasping at empty space. Or maybe they are still there but their affections have been redirected to another. Thus, the word "steadfast" has largely become devoid of meaning because experience has taught you that another person (perhaps even yourself) can stop loving anytime they see fit and for any number of frivolous and baseless reasons. If I can decide to love you, I can just as easily decide to stop. There's simply no guarantee that my love or yours will remain unalterable. The focus or object of a person's love may grow old and ugly, and the passion that once existed simply grows cold and dry. For others, it may be that their professed "love" has become conditional—with strings attached—and you find yourself in a relationship that feels demanding and dysfunctional.

The Rare Jewel of Steadfast Love

Steadfast love is in short supply. It always has been. That's not to say no one has experienced it. I have. For over fifty years my wife has steadfastly loved me and I have done my darndest to love her in like fashion. Of course, both of us would admit that there are times when love is hard to come by. It doesn't always flow freely or passionately. Our marriage has had its low moments just like everyone else's. But I would still use the word "steadfast" to describe our relationship.

That being said, many are still waiting and hoping and praying for someone whose love for them will remain steady, constant, and passionate. The worst part of it all is that sick, sinking feeling in your gut when a love you thought would never fail you turns out to be a fiction, a fantasy, a man-made hallucination. There are numerous relational failures that can inflict deep damage on the human heart. One thinks immediately of the love of a mother or father you had grown accustomed to but then watched it fade into the shadows as one or the other—or worse still, both—walked out and never returned. No one can survive in the absence of friendships, but they are also a precarious lot. A broken confidence. A subtle betrayal. A back turned. What you once were convinced was rock solid turned out to be as fleeting as a leaf blown in a summer breeze. And it hurts—badly. The result is often a determination to never trust anyone again.

There's something about being abandoned, undermined, or lied to by the one person who pledged to always love you that hurts beyond anything in comparison. This is what makes it so hard for people to take seriously the repeated affirmations in Scripture that God's love is steadfast. "Why should he be any different from everyone else?" we ask ourselves. What reason do I have to place my trust in God's love if the people he created and redeemed and calls his own so frequently fail to remain steadfast in their love? I can certainly understand this response. At one level, it makes perfectly good sense.

We think we know what the word "steadfast" means. After all, what other term could be descriptive of the Rock of Gibraltar or the soaring peaks of the Swiss Alps? And yet, when compared with the love of God for his people, Gibraltar is little more than a pebble tossed aimlessly by the waves of the ocean. The highest mountain in Switzerland is more akin to a feather being blown in the wind when set alongside the steadfastness of God's love. The Father's love for his children is immutable, unchangeable, enduring, unyielding, unalterable, constant, undeviating, and eternally fixed.

Even if you can't define the word "steadfast," you know it when you see it. It appears when the person you called on the phone for advice actually answers and helps. You see it when a friend shows up at the emergency room to check on you after a devastating car wreck. Steadfast has meaning and substance when your rent comes due and you can't pay it but your buddy happily places a check in your hand that will cover this month and the next two as well.

"If only God's commitment to us were as stable and constant," you think. But it is. In fact, it is far more reliable than any promise from a spouse or cousin or parent or next-door neighbor. And trusting in it does more to supply you with the strength to endure than any drug, artificial boost, or word of encouragement from a close acquaintance. Broken promises and betrayals in a marriage or a friendship threaten to diminish, if not entirely destroy, the love that once flourished. But not with God! God has shown his love "in that while we were still sinners, Christ died for us" (Rom. 5:8). Our willful rebellion and unbelief and idolatry and immoral conduct were no barrier to the consummate expression of God's love as seen in the gift of his Son. It is "while" (or at the very same time as) we continued to live in sin that God lovingly gave his Son on the cross for us.

Steadfast Love in the Psalms

If you doubt what I'm saying, let's take a minute or two to walk through the psalms of the Old Testament and reflect on what they say about God's steadfast love.

"Steadfast love" is our English translation of a single Hebrew word, *hesed*, used some 242 times in the Old Testament. On occasion it is translated as "mercy" or "lovingkindness" (as found in the New American Standard Bible [NASB]) or "goodness" or simply "love" (as in the New International Version [NIV]), and sometimes "loyal love." The adjective "steadfast" shows that this isn't a fleeting affection, momentary infatuation, or divine crush.

This word most often refers to the love that God has for his people as expressed in the context of his covenant with them (Ps. 89:28). Thus, some translate it as "covenant loyalty." Even in the midst of Israel's rebellion in the wilderness, "for their sake [God] remembered his covenant, and relented according to the abundance of his steadfast love" (Ps. 106:45). Ethan the Ezrahite, one of many psalmists, reassures us all of God's promise when he writes, "I will not remove from him my steadfast love or be false to my faithfulness. I will not violate my covenant or alter the word that went forth from my lips" (Ps. 89:33–34). Oh, how immeasurably different that is from even the love of a good friend, family member, or spouse! God's covenant with his people is sealed with blood, first as shed by a literal lamb on the Day of Atonement and later fulfilled by the death of the true and consummate Lamb of God, Jesus Christ, and his substitutionary sacrifice on the cross (John 1:29).

It's critically important that we never think of God's steadfast love only as a theological idea, notion, or principle. Each time it is used in the Psalter it is the motivation for worship and thanksgiving, the grounds for joy and peace, the power for perseverance, or the assurance of what awaits us in the future. Steadfast love is eminently practical. It is meant to strengthen and sustain our souls in the midst of the worst circumstances. God wants this truth about his commitment to us to reverberate in our hearts in every situation, no matter how dire or distressing they may be.

One of the first things we see in the Psalms is how God's steadfast love is so vastly different from the sappy sentimentalism we encounter in life today. The psalmist declares, "But I, through the abundance of your steadfast love, will enter your house. I will bow down toward your holy temple in the fear of you" (Ps. 5:7). Whoa; wait a minute! How can David speak of experiencing God's steadfast love at the same time he bows down before God in "fear"? Don't love and fear cancel out each other? How can they both exist simultaneously in the same heart? Won't one suffer at the altar of the other? Evidently not! David deeply felt the reassurance and security that comes from being the object of God's steadfast love and yet trembled in profound awe and amazement at the holiness and majesty of the God who loves him steadfastly. He genuinely feared the God who loved him. Because of this love, he knew that the God who is a consuming fire would never abandon him or turn him over to his enemies.

We often wonder about what God's ultimate motivation is in loving us the way he does. Why would he go to such self-sacrificial lengths to secure our salvation and adoption as his children? Again,

David has an answer: "Turn, O Lord, deliver my life; save me for the sake of your steadfast love" (Ps. 6:4; see 44:26). David's deepest desire is not primarily that he would be delivered but that, in such deliverance, God's steadfast love would be put on display as glorious, unchanging, and pure. It is "for the sake of" that love that David longs for protection and deliverance. His personal safety is of secondary importance. Preeminent in his heart is that God's love would be extolled and admired by all. That isn't to say that David isn't grateful for God's saving mercy. He later declares that he has "trusted" in God's "steadfast love" to uphold him in the face of his enemies, which leads his heart to rejoice in God's salvation (Ps. 13:5; see 17:7; 21:7). He again says, "Not to us, O Lord, not to us, but to your name give glory, for the sake of your steadfast love and your faithfulness" (Ps. 115:1).

In what is perhaps the most famous psalm he wrote, David finds deep encouragement in knowing that God's "mercy and goodness [*hesed*] shall follow" him all the days of his life (Ps. 23:6). Nothing is so unnerving as looking into the rearview mirror and seeing the flashing lights of a highway patrolman in fast pursuit of you and your car. But David loves the thought that if he ever were to look back over his shoulder, even when walking "through the valley of the shadow of death" (Ps. 23:4), he would see the blazing fire not of an impending speeding fine but the very goodness and steadfast love of God tailing him in order to protect, provide, and encourage, wherever he might go.

Do you ever find yourself in the grip of fear and anxiety that perhaps God's love has run dry in your time of need? King David probably wrestled with this as we do, but he reassured himself by calling on God to "remember [his] mercy" and "steadfast love, for they have been from of old" (Ps. 25:6). This remarkable love of

God was present in the past and David is assured that God will never fail to remember to supply it yet again in the present and on every day that is to follow.

But will not God instead remember our failures and have constantly in his mind our many sins and stumbles? David's prayer must be ours as well: "Remember not the sins of my youth or my transgressions; according to your steadfast love remember me, for the sake of your goodness, O Lord!" (Ps. 25:7). It isn't according to David's good deeds, promises he made, or sacrifices he contributed. No. Neither is it his repeated failures, sins, and shortcomings. The foundation or basis for David's assurance of God's continued presence in his life is the "steadfast love" and "goodness" of God!

How often do you think of God's steadfast love? Occasionally? Weekly? Perhaps rarely, if at all? David pledges to the Lord to keep his "steadfast love" ever "before [his] eyes" (Ps. 26:3). I can well imagine that as he awakened each day, one of the first things he prayed and committed himself to was keeping the reality of God's steadfast love firmly in his sight.

If David was anything, he was a worshiper of God. The psalms are flooded with his declarations of praise and thanksgiving and adoration. Typical of his time in worship is Psalm 31:7 where he declares, "I will rejoice and be glad in your steadfast love, because you have seen my affliction; you have known the distress of my soul" (see Ps. 52:8; 101:1). The love of God does not guarantee that we will never experience affliction or distress. Rather, it is in the midst of such adversity that we can be reassured that God's love remains and is steadfast and deserving of our trust (see Ps. 32:10). Does this attitude characterize your worship?

"Blessed be the Lord," David again sings in gratitude, "for he has wondrously shown his steadfast love to me when I was in a besieged city" (Ps. 31:21; see 31:16). David is determined to sing and celebrate God's "steadfast love in the morning" (Ps. 59:16) and throughout the day. Hear his resolute heart: "I will sing of the steadfast love of the LORD, forever; with my mouth I will make known your faithfulness to all generations. For I said, 'Steadfast love will be built up forever; in the heavens you will establish your faithfulness" (Ps. 89:1–2).

I suppose it is only natural for us to question the duration of God's love. Sadly, we often fall into despair, convinced that we've arrived at a place or time in life where God's steadfast love is largely if not wholly absent. But the psalmist thinks otherwise. "The steadfast love of God endures all the day" (Ps. 52:1). More than all the day, "his steadfast love endures *forever*" (Ps. 100:5). In fact, God loves "righteousness and justice; the earth is full of the steadfast love of the LORD" (Ps. 33:5). Think of that word "full." It is a much-needed reminder that there is no place where we might travel or live that God's steadfast love cannot be found in abundance. God is everywhere, and where God is, so too is his steadfast love for his children. But think of this: his steadfast love is not only everywhere present on the earth, it also "extends to the heavens" and his "faithfulness to the clouds" (Ps. 36:5; see 57:10; 108:4).

Hope is a strange and slippery notion. Hope, as found in Scripture, is far and away different from merely wishing that something good will happen. It is the rock-solid assurance that whatever God has promised us will undoubtedly come to pass. Yet, hope does not merely fix itself on the person of God or his promises but on his steadfast love as well! And oh how God loves it when we put our hope in that steadfast, immovable, and immutable love: "Behold, the eye of the LORD is on those who fear him, on those who hope in his steadfast love" (Ps. 33:18). Few things are as reassuring as knowing that wherever I go and whatever I do, God fixes his eye on me when I put my hope in his steadfast love. Again, only four verses later we read, "Let your steadfast love, O LORD, be upon us, even as we hope in you" (Ps. 33:22). The psalmist envisions God's love as more than something to be seen, known, or trusted. It is assuredly all that, but it is also a reality that we pray would rest "upon us," hovering above our heads, following us as the sun at day and the moon at night.

There are many things in my life that I regard as precious. I would begin with my wife of more than a half a century, my children and grandchildren, my extended family members, my brothers and sisters in Christ, my local church, and my books! Other things are precious in terms of their monetary value. And we take extraordinary steps to protect and preserve what we regard as precious, as having a value that calls for relentless oversight. We might even lock it away in a safety-deposit box at the bank or bury it in the backyard. But all else pales in comparison with the steadfast love of God. Nothing is more valuable. And we need not fear that a thief can steal it, a tornado destroy it, or a falling stock market empty it of its worth. David said it best when he proclaimed, "How precious is your steadfast love, O God!" (Ps. 36:7) and "Because your steadfast love is better than life, my lips will praise you" (Ps. 63:3). Yes, better than life or anything in it that we might think is of greater worth.

What dominates your conversation with friends, family, and even with those you barely know? Is it only the latest news, the most recent conflict somewhere in the earth, or perhaps the victory of your favorite athletic team? When David was with the people of God, one thing consumed him: "I have not hidden your deliverance within my heart; I have spoken of your faithfulness and your salvation; I have not concealed your steadfast love and your faithfulness from the great congregation" (Ps. 40:10). There are countless things we strive to conceal: our failures, facial blemishes, shame, disappointments, and so on. But may we never remain silent about God's steadfast love. God help us to proclaim it loudly in the presence of the great congregation! Yes, "by day the LORD commands his steadfast love, and at night his song is with me, a prayer to the God of my life" (Ps. 42:8; see 48:9; 57:3). What song is this? What prayer? It concerns the "steadfast love" of God that he himself commands "by day" to be with me.

Most Christians are familiar with Psalm 51. There we read of David's heartfelt repentance for his sin with Bathsheba and his complicity in the murder of her husband, Uriah the Hittite. It is a passionate plea for mercy and forgiveness. But to what does David appeal as the basis for God's favor? His service as king over Israel? His courageous defeat of Goliath? His many military victories? No. "Have mercy on me, O God, according to your steadfast love; according to your abundant mercy blot out my transgressions" (Ps. 51:1; see 109:26). David dares not come to God with a resume of earthly achievements or accolades. Nothing in his past or his future is cited as the grounds for his restoration to the heart of God. It is the latter's steadfast love alone to which David looks, and so should we.

One of the more debilitating fears that Christians encounter is what they perceive to be the potential loss of God's favor and presence. Their sin weighs heavily on their hearts and they can't shake free of the thought that God will simply up and leave them. That is why it is so important for us to meditate deeply on the reality of God's steadfast love. "Blessed be God," declared the psalmist, "because he has not rejected my prayer or removed his steadfast love from me!" (Ps. 66:20). And he never will.

The psalmist's confidence that God will hear his prayers is reiterated by David: "But as for me, my prayer is to you, O LORD. At an acceptable time, O God, in the abundance of your steadfast love answer me in your saving faithfulness" (Ps. 69:13). How reassuring it is to know that God's steadfast love exists in "abundance"! God is never in short supply of his covenantal affection for his children. And it is precisely because of this overflowing and effusive abundance of steadfast love that he answers us when we cry out to him.

Again, David brings his prayer to God: "Answer me, O LORD, for your steadfast love is good; according to your abundant mercy, turn to me" (Ps. 69:16). Yes, his love is good. Yes, his mercy is abundant. Never live in fear that when you turn to God you will find him empty-handed. How do I know this? I know it because God is "good and forgiving, abounding in steadfast love to all who call upon" him (Ps. 86:5; see 89:14, 24; 117:2; 118:1–4, 29). His steadfast love is "great" (Ps. 86:13) and more than adequate to meet our every need.

What do you need to sustain your heart with gladness and joy? What will ultimately satisfy your soul? More money? A better job? More robust health? When you wake up each day, what is the first thing that enters your thoughts? Do you live in anticipation of a job you finally secured after years of education? Or is it in anticipation of meeting an old friend for lunch after years of separation? Do you think of how you will spend the evening once the day has passed? What is it that you look to and hope for that you are convinced will satisfy the deepest longings of your soul? All those things just noted are good. They are among God's many gifts to us. But hear the prayer of the psalmist: "Satisfy us in the morning with your steadfast love, that we may rejoice and be glad all our days" (Ps. 90:14). The world around us, and far too many Christians as well, hanker after every possible pleasure and believe every unimaginable lie that assures us we need more of this and more of that if we ever hope to find joy and gladness. But God's word is clear and unmistakable: the experience of God's *hesed* is the only all-sufficient source of true joy and the sort of gladness that will keep us far from sin.

What do you think it is that keeps you from slipping and falling away from God's saving presence? I can assure you, as I do myself, that it isn't in our willpower or New Year's resolutions. It is God's love. As the psalmist says, "When I thought, 'My foot slips,' your steadfast love, O LORD, held me up" (Ps. 94:18). God's commitment to preserve you fully and finally unto the last day and deliver you safely into his eternal kingdom is rooted in his steadfast love for you.

Many point to Psalm 103 as their favorite psalm, as the one hymn that powerfully reinforces the truth of God's forgiveness and longsuffering. And to what do we attribute this attitude he takes toward broken people like you and me? David put it this way: he "redeems your life from the pit" and "crowns you with steadfast love and mercy" (Ps. 103:4). Steadfast love a crown? As strange as the imagery may be, it is still the case that God crowns our heads with his fatherly affection. He is "merciful and gracious, slow to anger and abounding in steadfast love" (Ps. 103:8). How high, how expansive, how incalculably great is God's love for you and me? "As high as the heavens are above the earth, so great is his steadfast love toward those who fear him" (Ps. 103:11). And just when someone tries to tell you there's a limit to all good things, God reminds us that his "steadfast love" is "from everlasting to everlasting on those who fear him" (Ps. 103:17; see 106:1; 107:1).

The apostle Paul describes Father God as the source and power behind all comfort (2 Cor. 1:3–4). But how does he do this? Among other ways, it is through the promise of his steadfast love as the psalmist says: "Let your steadfast love comfort me according to your promise to your servant" (Ps. 119:76). As if that were not enough, the psalmist continues to pray that in God's "steadfast love" he will give him "life" so that he may have strength to "keep the testimonies of [God's] mouth" (Ps. 119:88; see 119:149, 159).

Many struggle to think that God actually enjoys his people, that he takes pleasure and finds delight in them. Count me among them! But then I am reminded that "the LORD takes pleasure in those who fear him, in those who hope in his steadfast love" (Ps. 147:11). There is hardly anything that more readily brings a smile to your heavenly Father's face than your determination to hope in his steadfast love. Your present confidence that God is for you and your expectations for a good future are rooted in God's commitment to seek your best and most blessed welfare, to never to leave you or forsake you.

We hear much today from critics of contemporary worship music that it can, at times, be rather repetitive. And they are often right. But repetition isn't always a bad thing. One need only read Psalm 136 to see this is true. No fewer than twenty-six times in this psalm is the endurance and undying nature of God's steadfast love affirmed. It serves as the refrain following each declaration of some act of sovereign mercy, deliverance, judgment, or provision. Three times in the first three verses we are exhorted to "give thanks to the LORD," to the "God of gods," to the "Lord of lords" (Ps. 136: 1, 2, 3). And the reason given for this, each time, is that "his steadfast love endures forever" (vv. 1, 2, 3).

What follows in this remarkable psalm is a rehearsal of all the mighty deeds of God on behalf of his people, and each case is attributed to the simple but glorious truth that God's steadfast love endures forever. Whether it is his miracle-working power in performing "great wonders" (136:4), his creation of the "heavens" above (v. 5) or his making "the great lights"—namely, the sun (v. 8), the moon, and innumerable stars (v. 9)—the reason for our gratitude is that his steadfast love endures forever!

In verses 10–16 the psalmist briefly recalls the many mighty deeds of God in delivering Israel from their bondage in Egypt, all because of the steadfast love that he had for them. In verses 17–22, reference is made to the many kings and military opponents God overthrew to demonstrate how his steadfast love for his people endures forever. Be it his remembrance of us "in our low estate" (v. 23) or the many ways in which he has "rescued us from our foes" (v. 24), the refrain is wonderfully the same: "for his steadfast love endures forever."

I think the Psalms alone are sufficient to justify the writing of a book on God's steadfast love. If we hear and understand only a fraction of what the psalmists say about it, we will come away rejoicing just like they did.

3

Sovereign Love on Bended Knee

ENVISION YOURSELF in the most painful situation imaginable. Your finances are in a shambles, your health is deteriorating daily, and you are all alone. No one seems to care how you feel. You have a splitting headache, the house is an unmitigated mess, and tomorrow has all the signs of being worse than today. Then, the telephone rings. Sure enough, it's that one person in your life who never calls or seems to care until they need something from you. And today, of all days, you're in no condition to give. How would you react?

As bad as that scenario may sound, it is nothing compared to what Jesus was facing as he sat with his disciples in the upper room. Jesus was only hours away from being abandoned, deserted, and denied by those who loudly proclaimed their loyalty to him. He was facing the most excruciating crisis of his earthly life. He was already aware of the treachery of Judas Iscariot slowly creeping up behind him. He could smell Satan's hideous breath in his face. He could see the lurking shadow of the cross and the shame that lay ahead.

If it were you or I in that situation, I suspect we would have loudly complained about our need for ministry, encouragement, and the attention of those we thought cared about us. But not Jesus. At that precise moment, unlike you and me, Jesus could only think of others. And these weren't just any "others"—they were the men who would shortly turn their backs on him, shamefully forsake him in utter cowardice, and leave him all alone to face his executioners.

Do you want to know what Jesus thinks about people like that? Are you curious about what he feels for individuals who will soon treat him this way? Do you wonder what he is willing to do for such folk? I do, because I'm just like them. Had I been in their sandals, I would no doubt have done precisely what they did. I'm sure I would have loudly proclaimed my commitment, love, and undying devotion to Jesus. And I'm also fairly certain that when everything began to fall apart and the pressure was on, I would have run away like a whipped, frightened puppy, concerned only for my own welfare and indifferent toward his.

There are two parts to this chapter of our book. To start, we will look at three things in John 13:1–11 that might appear to be insurmountable obstacles to Jesus loving his own. Taking note of these factors magnifies his love beyond comprehension. After this, we'll examine four characteristics of the love that Jesus had for his disciples, things that equally characterize his love for us now. But first, it's crucial that you pause and read John 13:1–11:

> Now before the Feast of the Passover, when Jesus knew that his hour had come to depart out of this world to the Father, having loved his own who were in the world, he loved them to the end. During supper, when the devil had already put it into the heart of Judas Iscariot, Simon's son, to betray him, Jesus, knowing that the Father had given all things into his hands, and that

he had come from God and was going back to God, rose from supper. He laid aside his outer garments, and taking a towel, tied it around his waist. Then he poured water into a basin and began to wash the disciples' feet and to wipe them with the towel that was wrapped around him. He came to Simon Peter, who said to him, "Lord, do you wash my feet?" Jesus answered him, "What I am doing you do not understand now, but afterward you will understand." Peter said to him, "You shall never wash my feet." Jesus answered him, "If I do not wash you, you have no share with me." Simon Peter said to him, "Lord, not my feet only but also my hands and my head!" Jesus said to him, "The one who has bathed does not need to wash, except for his feet, but is completely clean. And you are clean, but not every one of you." For he knew who was to betray him; that was why he said, "Not all of you are clean."

Three Seemingly Insurmountable Obstacles to Love

The first potential obstacle to Jesus's love in this passage is that things seem to be totally out of control, running amok, almost as if Jesus himself is being swept away by the swift march of events, like objects being carried away by the rapidly rising rushing waters of the Mississippi. Satan is beginning his assault on Judas Iscariot, prompting him to betray Jesus. The Jewish religious leaders are plotting against him. Pontius Pilate, Herod, and the crowds in the city are all postured to contribute their part to his eventual crucifixion. It almost seems as if history itself is slipping through God's fingers! But this is no barrier to Jesus loving his own, for at no time did he ever lose control over himself or the events of history. He knows who he is, where he has come from, what he's going to do, how much it will cost, and who he is going to once it's all over.

At no time during his earthly life, at no time during your earthly life, does Jesus cease to be sovereign. From tornadoes and terrorist bombings to beheadings, the rise and fall of the stock market, deteriorating health, the confusion and turmoil of an impending presidential election, or the rebellion of a child, our Lord is ever in control. All that was made by him is still sustained through him and will ultimately prove to be for him.

Crawl with me, as it were, inside the head of Jesus. John tells us what he was thinking and feeling in this crucial hour—"Jesus knew that his hour had come to depart out of this world to the Father" (13:1). As a grammar geek, I love possessive pronouns, and they figure prominently in this passage. Jesus knew that "his" hour had come. Jesus loved "his" own who were in the world. God had given all things into "his" hands. What a glorious word, a comforting and reassuring word.

Now, why do I say that? This first use of the word "his" reminds us that what was about to transpire didn't surprise Jesus or catch him off guard. This is what he was born to do. The hour decreed by his Father has arrived. Neither the Romans' political maneuverings nor the Jewish leaders' religious scheming could derail, disrupt, or delay "his hour" from coming. God is in absolute control. Until now, the religious leaders and Roman military could lay nary a hand on him. But now "his" hour had come. The time had finally come for the Son of Man to be delivered up, voluntarily and joyfully, into the hands of his enemies.

We so often think that the swirl of world events and the ever-increasing series of tragedies that confront us daily are a surprise to God or perhaps so engage and entangle him that he forgets about us. No! The greatest crisis of all human history is about to unfold, namely, the crucifixion of the Son of Man, and yet in the midst of it all he is thinking about his own. As much as Jesus might appear to be in the grip of his enemies, they themselves are firmly in the grip of God who is working all things according to his sovereign purpose. Such is the steadfast love of Jesus for "his own."

The second potential obstacle to Jesus's love as seen in this passage is power and authority. When people are promoted and praised and find themselves in a position of authority, they tend to forget others. They are absorbed in their own achievements, they are enamored of their own press clippings, and all others suddenly become expendable and less important. Admit it: it's hard to be passionately concerned for others when your head is swelled with thoughts of your own importance. But not Jesus.

Look again at verse 3—Jesus *knew* that "the Father had given all things into his hands." By "all things" he had in mind not just the disciples, who loved and followed him, but also Judas Iscariot, who was about to betray him. All of these were his to do with as he pleased. Satan was his to do with as he pleased. Pontius Pilate and Herod and all the rulers of both Rome and Israel were his to do with as he pleased. And with all the power of heaven and earth at his disposal, he chose to think of his own. Remember, he said he could have called twelve legions of angels to deliver him if he wanted (Matt. 26:53). But even with the authority to blast Judas and Satan and Pontius Pilate into the next galaxy, he thinks only of his own. Such is the steadfast love of our Savior.

Try to imagine the disciples sitting around the table that night, looking intently at the face of Jesus. What was racing through their minds? Perhaps questions like "What's he thinking about?" and "What's on his mind?" I'll tell you exactly what he was thinking about. Jesus was saying to himself something like, "It's all mine!

I am the Lord and sovereign king over everything. My Father has put all things in my hands."

His mind was filled with thoughts of the power, dominion, authority, glory, and honor that he would receive from his Father. And it was precisely then, at that very moment, with images and ideas of his authority swirling around in his head, that he rose from supper, girded himself with a towel, got down on his knees, and washed his disciples' feet (John 13:4–5)! Instead of letting thoughts of his own greatness exempt him from serving others, instead of using the truth of his own preeminence and power to justify ignoring their needs, instead of letting his own exalted position lead him to think that this ragtag group of sinners was beneath his dignity as Lord of the universe, he loved and served them by washing their feet.

It's breathtaking, is it not? In the midst of such indescribable turmoil and impending arrest and crucifixion, all he could think about was loving and serving his "own." Such is the steadfast love of our Lord.

The third potential obstacle to Jesus's love in this passage is his knowledge of his origin and destination. Often, when we consider where we've come from and where we're going, we turn our thoughts inward to self and away from any focus on or concern for others. Some people think that since they come from aristocracy, they have no business mingling with, much less serving, the lower classes of society.

Not Jesus. Look again at John 13:3. Jesus was thinking about how "he had come from God" and "was going back to God." Clearly this refers to his thoughts concerning his preincarnate glory and majesty and the mutual love between the Father and Spirit in the fellowship of the Godhead (see John 17:1–5). Perhaps he is thinking of the echo of angelic praise. Perhaps he's reflecting on the adoring worship of the four living creatures or the sustained cry of "Holy, holy, holy" coming from stunned seraphim surrounding his throne (Rev. 4:8). It may also be a reference to his sense of divine mission. It certainly refers to his expectation of being exalted once again to that place and experience of glory that his state of humiliation had temporarily interrupted.

And yet, knowing full well who he was, knowing and reflecting on the glory that was his from eternity past, the glory that would be his for eternity future, he *still* chose to think about others—his own. John couldn't have been any clearer: while such thoughts were swirling around in Jesus's head, he was fixated on the steadfast love he had for his own (John 13:1).

Four Characteristics of Jesus's Steadfast Love for His Own

Now that we've seen how Jesus's love of his own was not derailed by situational chaos, his sense of power and authority, or his knowledge of returning to the Father, we can look at four characteristics of this love. First, we read in verse 1 that "having loved his own who were in the world, he loved them to the end." What's the point of describing his disciples as being "in the world"? It seems so obvious, so trite. Of course they are in the world. Where else could they be? Surely, something more is intended by this phrase.

I believe it is John's way of magnifying the love of Christ by highlighting the disciples' unloveliness. Jesus didn't wait for them to experience final glorification in heaven before he loved them. He didn't suspend his love for them on their perfection, sinlessness, spotlessness, purity, or expulsion of all those annoying habits and personality quirks that would otherwise make them unfit for love.

Rather, Jesus loved his own in the midst of their weakness, immaturity, ignorance, and brokenness. And he loves you in the midst of yours as well! As his eyes glanced around the room, he saw men whose failures were obvious, yet he loved them. There was Matthew who probably still struggled with greed, who perhaps still lamented leaving such a high paying job to follow Jesus. Then there was Andrew, possibly dealing with lingering resentment against his brother Peter for being so prominent among the disciples and being chosen to be part of the inner circle. And I hardly need to comment on Peter's repeated failures and impulsive actions. Jesus knew them all. He knew everything about them. He knew things deep in their souls that not even they had discovered: their secret sins, fears, and longings.

They were still in the world and the world, to a certain extent, was still in them. But he still loved them. Don't miss this point. It wasn't in anticipation of their final deliverance from sin and corruption that he loved them. He didn't glance at their sin, weakness, and frailty and say, "Well, one day they'll be loveable. One day they'll finally live up to my expectations. One day they'll deserve my affection." No, he loved them then, while they were yet in the world, while they were yet weak, immature, broken, and unwilling to stand by him in his hour of greatest need.

Do you struggle to believe that God truly loves you now? Are you inclined to think that he will only love you once you've broken free from your sinful addictions, cleaned your house, received a substantial pay raise at work, and overcome all your sinful habits, pride, doubts and bitterness? Jesus knew the disciples' sinful fantasies and he knows yours as well. He knew their arrogant ambitions and anxieties, and he knows yours as well. But he kept on loving them while they were yet in the world, and he will keep on loving you while you are in the world!

Second, John 13:1 says that Jesus "loved them to the end." The NIV renders this phrase as "He showed them the full extent of his love," meaning love in its highest intensity. But I believe the word "end" more likely refers to Jesus's impending death—meaning something like he loved them "to his last breath" or "all the way to the cross." In spite of all that he was about to endure, he never stopped loving them. And he will never stop loving you. His love is truly steadfast!

In any case, the point is that he never grew weary in his love for them. His love never wavered, never weakened, never waned. When he most needed to receive love, he gave love. With every reason in the world not to love the disciples, at least from a human perspective, he loved them all the way to the end: unendingly, unceasingly, incessantly, without pause or hesitation or a second thought.

Think of it. Peter is about to deny him three times. All the others are about to run off into the night, frightened beyond words, leaving him to face his accusers alone. Dare I say that you and I would have acted in the same way? And yet his love for them (and for us) continued, unchanged and undiminished, all the way to the end.

Third, John 13:1 describes those whom Jesus loved as "his own"—his own peculiar and personal possession. They are "his own" because they were given to him by his Father and he will redeem them by his blood (see John 6:37–39; 10:29; 17:2; 1 Cor. 6:19–20). Although he is the sovereign proprietor over all things, he has a special affection for his own.

I find it significant that it doesn't say he loved "his disciples" or "his followers" or "believers" or "his sheep" or even "his friends." They and we are here described as "his own"! You who don't feel you belong to anyone else, you are his own. You who live alone and doubt if anyone cares, you are his own. You who live in fear that you may never achieve anything of significance in this life or think of yourself as a complete failure, you are his own. You who often wonder aloud, "Why would anyone ever want me?" are his own. The Creator of heaven and earth regards you as his own. You may find yourself saying, "I'm not much in the eyes of others, but when it comes to Jesus, I'm his own."

Whether you are in the office or at school, down in the dumps, over the hill, driving a car, or eating your breakfast, you are now and ever will be his own! You may hate your job or be wondering if your spouse will ever love you the way you hoped they would. You may never read your name in the local newspaper, be quoted on the internet, or hold office in the church. But you are now and ever his own. I have no way of providing you with a guarantee that your health, finances, or relationship status will ever change, but I can guarantee, now and forever, that if you believe in Jesus, you are his own!

Were ever more precious and endearing words spoken? Was there ever a more glorious privilege, a more exalted position, a more intimate relationship?

Fourth, John 13:4–11 shows us that Jesus's love was not merely an inward affection but made itself known by an unexpected and socially offensive expression. Here is Jesus thinking of eternal glory, exaltation, power, and authority. And what does he do? Does he bark out commands like "Peter, bring me my purple robe. John, my scepter. Matthew, my golden crown. Phillip, dust off my throne"? No. He washed their feet.

Everything was in place. The pitcher, the basin, the water, the towel. But no one moved. Not so much as a stirring. Each man would have looked at the others, holding their breath, wondering who was going to take the initiative, and secretly hoping it would not fall on his own shoulders.

Most of us are familiar with the custom of foot washing, even those who have never actually participated in it. I was raised a Southern Baptist and had only heard of the practice existing among other, so-called "primitive" Baptists. But during my four years at Wheaton College, my wife and I were members of an Anglican church that observed this ritual once each year during holy week. The first time I attended the service, I chose not to participate. I didn't know what to do and hadn't given much thought to its significance, so I abstained. And to be honest, I was a bit uncomfortable with something so intimate and new.

The next year I was determined to participate, so I made all the adequate preparations. I washed my feet as thoroughly as I ever had! I made certain to select clean socks and even put a little sweet-smelling powder in my shoes. The last thing I wanted was to offend some unsuspecting student of mine with a putrid odor.

How utterly unlike the first century! Without paved roads and concrete sidewalks, people in the ancient world were accustomed to the dirt, filth, and ugliness of walking all day in open-toed sandals. Washing another's feet was profoundly unpleasant. This is one reason it was a task assigned to the household slave. No one would ever have expected a member of the family, and far less a guest, to stoop so low as to wash another's feet.

But the principal objection to this act was less physical than social. Yes, it was physically distasteful. Make no mistake about that. But more important still was the social indignity of it all. As best we can tell, there isn't a single recorded instance in all of Jewish or Greco-Roman sources of a superior washing the feet of a subordinate—that is, until Jesus!

Suddenly, in the upper room, the last thing the disciples could possibly have expected happened. Jesus rose from his place, removed his outer garment, girded himself with a towel, knelt down, and began doing what was to their minds inconceivable and utterly inappropriate. Jesus was simply acting consistently with his own teaching: "I am among you as one who serves" (Luke 22:27).

In fact, it seems that Jesus even washed the feet of his worst and most faithless enemy, Judas Iscariot. Why do I say this? For starters, we know Judas was present when this incident took place because of what we read in John 13:21–30. Further, the text repeatedly refers to the "disciples" as a group without suggesting that Judas was an exception. And last, if Jesus had not washed the feet of Judas, then surely the others would have noticed and asked why or would not have gone on to ask in verse 25 who it was that would betray him as it would have been obvious from Judas's exclusion.

No, I can't prove beyond doubt that Jesus washed the feet of Judas. It is, after all, an argument from silence. But the evidence seems to weigh in favor of concluding he did.

So what does that tell us? Maybe Jesus was unaware of Judas's intent—he didn't know what Judas was planning on doing and thus washed his feet thinking he was as committed as Peter and John and the others. Or maybe Judas himself had not yet decided to betray Jesus. No; neither of these work. Although verse 2 doesn't say that Jesus already knew that Satan had put it into Judas's heart to betray him, verse 11 makes it clear that Jesus was aware of who the traitor was. Thus the washing of Judas's feet does not mean he was saved (see vv. 10–11). Does it suggest he was being given one last chance to repent? I don't know, but I doubt it.

Perhaps the point of Jesus's washing the feet of Judas (what must Judas have thought as he looked down into the eyes of Jesus as this happened?) was simply to demonstrate to us how we are to love our enemies. The next time you wonder how to relate to your worst enemy, the person who repeatedly slanders you, gossips about you, betrays you, and deceives you, picture in your mind Jesus, on hands and knees, washing the filthy feet of Judas Iscariot. Often we love and serve others only because we hope they will reciprocate. But Jesus knew the only thing he would ever receive back from Judas was betrayal.

Conclusion

How do you cope when everything in your life conspires to convince you that God couldn't possibly love anyone as wretched as you, anyone as much a failure as you perceive yourself to be? What is your response when, in the depths of your soul, you feel like a complete disaster and a constant disappointment to God? How do you manage? What strategy do you employ just to survive?

Are you the sort of person who puts on a smile, all the while suppressing the pain and resisting the temptation to run away from friends, family, and especially the church? Or are you the kind of individual who turns to the latest cultural gimmick, self-help formula, New York Times bestselling book, or whatever it is that Oprah is offering to help you feel good about yourself again?

If anything is clear to us from John 13, it is that there's a better way, a more satisfying solution, a more Christ-exalting answer to your self-doubts and the contempt you might feel for yourself. The answer is found in the unshakeable reality of God's steadfast love for you in Christ Jesus. You are his own, and he will love you all the way to the end, even though you are still in the world and the world is still in you.

I pray that this passage of Scripture might become an immovable rock of assurance and safety for you. I want it to become a safe haven, a refuge to which you can always retreat when the reality of God's love for you seems distant and far removed.

4

The Look of Steadfast Love

WHAT HAPPENS to God's steadfast love when we joyfully embrace and trust it, only to later return to our old habits of sin and selfishness?[1] We know this experience all too well. Each of us is deeply moved by the magnitude of God's love. Our hearts overflow with gratitude. We marvel that God would love people like you and me. Perhaps we break out in songs of praise and adoration. But then it happens—temptation comes, pressure mounts, and we cave to the impulses of our flesh and sin yet again, often in the same way as we did before.

Perhaps a real-life illustration of this scenario will help. We have one in the person of the apostle Peter. But to fully appreciate what he experienced and find in his personal journey hope for our own, we need to briefly rehearse the events of the final days of Jesus.

In chapter 3, we saw a vivid expression of the steadfast love of our Lord. While contemplating his sovereign sway over all creation, while reflecting on the glory of eternity past and the exaltation

---

1 This chapter has been adapted from my book *To Love Mercy: Becoming a Person of Compassion, Acceptance, and Forgiveness* (Colorado Springs: NavPress, 1991). Used by permission.

that awaited him in the future, Jesus demonstrated his love for his disciples in a countercultural and unexpected manner—he washed their feet. One would think that this should be enough to secure their faithfulness, obedience, and devotion. Surely, none present that night in the upper room would ever again gain the consent of their souls to sin against this kind of steadfast love. Well, think again.

After this event (John 13–17), Jesus entered into the agony of Gethsemane. He persevered, submitting his will to that of his Father. He drank the cup that was prepared for him, the cup of God's righteous wrath and judgment against those for whom he would give himself as a substitute on the cross.

As we've noted before, the arresting party laid their hands on him; they seized him, something that they attempted to do on numerous prior occasions but failed. They failed because, as Jesus said repeatedly, "My hour has not yet come" (John 2:4). But now his hour had arrived. The hour of his suffering for sinners had arrived. And so the invisible hand that had kept them at bay was lifted and Jesus was delivered over into their grasp.

We read in John 18 that Peter followed Jesus into the courtyard of the high priest. It was there that a servant girl approached him with words he feared he might hear. "Aren't you one of this man's disciples?" (see John 18:17). "No," responded Peter with no small measure of indignation. A few moments later, several servants and officers who were standing with Peter around a charcoal fire likewise said, "Wait a minute. Aren't you one of the disciples of Jesus?" He denied it again.

Earlier, while in Gethsemane with Jesus, Peter reacted impulsively and cut off the ear of a man named Malchus, the servant of the high priest. Now, one of Malchus's relatives was present around the fire when Peter was queried about his relationship with Jesus.

He recognized Peter and asked him a third time, "Didn't I see you in the garden with Jesus?" "No!" shouted Peter, no doubt wishing that everyone would simply leave him alone. And at once a rooster crowed.

For our purposes in this chapter, I'm going to ask each of you to try as best you can to put yourself in the place of Peter. I want you to see these events unfold from his perspective. And most of all, I want you to feel what he felt. Why, you ask? Because you will probably never fully understand the reality of the steadfast love of Christ and the magnitude of the forgiveness he provides until you do.

Is Forgiveness Possible?

Is forgiveness possible? It may sound like a silly question, especially to Christians who know what the Bible says about God's grace and redemption and the forgiveness of sin through faith in Christ. But even for Christians, sometimes "forgiveness" is just a word lost in a stack of abstract theological language that we recite in our church liturgies.

If you're anything like me, none of that matters if you can't receive forgiveness into the depths of your soul and experience its liberating, life-changing power and taste its sweetness. So let me ask the question again: Is forgiveness possible? Can a thief be forgiven? What about an adulterer? What about a woman who's had an abortion or a man who's paid for one? What about those failures, those sins, committed long ago, forgotten by everyone else but still lingering in our spiritual memory, sins whose guilt and shame we carry around tucked away safely in our hearts? Is forgiveness possible?

Why is it even important for us to answer this question? Simply because, as John Piper once said, the only sin that can be defeated is a sin that has been forgiven.[2] There are countless natural ways to overcome bad habits and repeated failures: therapies, formulas, willpower. But without divine forgiveness, they only produce human righteousness, not the righteousness of God. In other words, being right with God must precede doing right for God. That's why our question is so crucial. Let me answer the question by directing your attention to a story that many don't even know is in the Bible—when Jesus locked eyes with Peter after Peter's denial of his friendship.

All of us have been in situations when we were desperate for a friend, just one person to stand with us to face the hard things in life. Jesus was no exception. Earlier in his ministry, he had often wanted to be alone. He would quietly slip away while the others were sleeping, hungry for solitude, for that rare moment alone with the Father, away from the pressure of the crowds and the endless questioning of the Pharisees. The last thing he wanted was someone to interrupt and hang around.

But that was then. This is now—the night of his betrayal. "You will all fall away because of me this night," said Jesus (Matt. 26:31). Not just any night, but "this" very night, the night Jesus and the disciples sat together in the upper room and enjoyed a depth of personal and spiritual intimacy perhaps unlike anything they had known before. This very night—the night they ate, prayed, and sang together, experienced remarkable fellowship, love, and joy—they would all abandon him.

"You will be offended by me," Jesus told them. "Your faith will turn to fear. At first sight of the enemy you will all turn tail and scamper away into the shadows like so many frightened pups. For

---

2 This quotation is from the author's personal experience.

it is written, 'I will strike the shepherd, and the sheep of the flock will be scattered'" (see Matt. 26:31).

"Not me, Lord! No way!" Peter's protest was loud and arrogant. "Maybe John will abandon you. I mean, anyone so loving and tender has to be a little soft, a bit weak, especially when the chips are down. But not me! Not good old Peter! Hey, don't forget, Lord, I'm the rock. You said so yourself. Remember?"

You may be tempted to think that Peter declared his undying commitment to Jesus with his fingers crossed behind his back. Perhaps he was saying to himself, "I've got to make it look like I would never turn my back on the Savior. After all, I've got a reputation to uphold. But I've got to give myself an out, an excuse I can appeal to if things go haywire." I don't think so. It is far more likely that Peter could never envision failing to carry out his promise. This is confirmed by what we read in Matthew 26:58. There we are told that he "was following him at a distance, as far as the courtyard of the high priest, and going inside he sat with the guards to see the end." What could Peter possibly have been thinking? Why would he have followed Jesus into the enemy camp if he had any lingering concerns that he might deny Jesus?

Perhaps he had forgotten Jesus's prediction. Was it already a fading memory? That's doubtful, as it had only been a few hours before that Jesus spoke these ominous words, "Truly I tell you, this very night, before the rooster crows, you will deny me three times" (26:34).

Rather, hearing those words, Peter boldly begged to differ with Jesus. We can only imagine what more he might have said, or at least thought, in reaction to the dire prediction about him. Perhaps something like this: "I hear you, Lord. And I don't mean to sound argumentative. But I'll never disown you. I'll die first! I can't speak for the others. Some of them aren't as strong as I am. They didn't walk on water like me. Sure, I know you selected each of them, Lord, but don't forget that Matthew was a tax collector. It wouldn't surprise me if he reverted to his former ways. After all, greed and materialism aren't easily uprooted from the human heart. And I grew up with Andrew. If you only knew how often he's messed up. But not me, Lord. You can always count on old Peter!"

Instead of falling on his face and humbly pleading for grace to withstand the coming test, Peter implicitly accused Jesus of lying. But he wasn't alone in this, for "all the disciples said the same" (Matt. 26:35). We don't know what motivated them to chime in with Peter's protest. Perhaps they were sincere, or maybe they just didn't want to be outdone by Peter's declaration of love and loyalty. In any case, Jesus was right and they were wrong (see Matt. 26:56).

After this, the kangaroo court convened. Trumped-up charges. Lying witnesses. Accusations of blasphemy. Then the consummate indignity: "they spit in his face and struck him. And some slapped him, saying, 'Prophesy to us, you Christ! Who is it that struck you?'" (Matt. 26:67–68).

And where was Peter when Jesus needed him most? He was sitting outside in the courtyard, possibly puffed up with confidence in his own resolve to remain true to the Lord, looking for the opportunity to show himself to be right and Jesus wrong. He eventually made his way to a fire in order to warm himself along with several others who were present. When a servant girl came up to him and asked if he was one of the disciples of Jesus, surely Peter would have said to himself, "Finally. I've been waiting here patiently hoping someone would eventually recognize me and ask that question. Now I've got the opportunity to prove my point and demonstrate to everyone what I'm made of. At last, the chance to show how deep my loyalty runs and what kind of man I really am."

Well, apparently not. Matthew says that "he denied it before them all, saying 'I do not know what you mean'" (Matt. 26:70). It was a standoff: Peter, the rock, the strong-armed, grizzled fisherman, face-to-face with—a servant girl? Surely not!

Had Peter been confronted by Pontius Pilate and threatened with immediate execution, perhaps we might understand (though by no means excuse) his failure. If it were Caiaphas the high priest, Annas, or a Roman soldier with a sword pressed perilously close to Peter's throat, we could understand. But a servant girl?

Frustrated and fearful, Peter sought an avenue of escape. He went out to the gateway but was again confronted, this time by— you guessed it—"another servant girl" (Matt. 26:71). She said to the people there, "This man was with Jesus of Nazareth" (Matt. 26:71). But Peter "denied it with an oath: 'I do not know the man!'" (26:72).

When challenged yet a third time, Peter "began to invoke a curse on himself and to swear, 'I do not know the man!'" (Matt. 26:74). He not only invoked a solemn curse on himself should he be lying but also on his accusers should they persist in bringing such charges against him. Peter didn't use profanity, as some have thought. His oath was in all likelihood an appeal to something sacred, used to reinforce the truth of his denial. Perhaps he said, "By all that is holy, I swear I don't know the man!" or "With God as my witness, this man is a stranger to me!" or "I appeal to the sacred city Jerusalem that I am telling you the truth about him!" Adding insult to injury, he even refused to use the name of Jesus. He contemptuously, disdainfully, and cowardly referred to him as "the man." How far he had fallen from that monumental confession, "You are the Christ, the Son of the Living God" (Matt. 16:16).

But let's be clear about one thing. My detailed portrayal of Peter's sin is not designed to hold him up for public ridicule. I understand all too well Peter's weakness. Don't we all? Why, then, have I gone to such lengths to describe his self-protective cowardice? I did it so that you and I might grasp the magnitude of God's steadfast love for us and in turn might more readily love and forgive those who have betrayed us and sinned against us.

There are two remarkable events in Peter's story that make this point. At the beginning of this story, all four Gospel authors record the crowing of the rooster. Luke alone, the beloved physician, tells us that in the wake of Peter's third denial, perhaps just as the rooster crowed, "the Lord turned and looked at Peter" (Luke 22:61). We can't be certain how much time passed between Peter's denial and the moment when Jesus looked at him. Probably no more than seconds. But honestly, it doesn't really matter. It was just enough time for Peter to feel the force of his failure.

Pause for a moment and consider the majesty of divine providence. Consider how God the Father orchestrated this moment with such precision and beauty. There must have been dozens of people everywhere, running back and forth, caught up in the frenzy of the events of that night. Yet Jesus saw only Peter, and Peter saw only Jesus. Jesus is being shuttled back and forth, dragged through courtyards and in and out of rooms. Peter's loud cursing still echoed in the courtyard of Caiaphas. Yet at precisely the moment the rooster crowed, the Father providentially arranged for Jesus and Peter to be in sight of each other. Jesus turned and locked eyes with Peter! And then Peter "remembered the saying of the Lord, how he had said to him, 'Before the rooster crows today, you will deny me three times.' And he went out and wept bitterly" (Luke 22:61–62).

Peter's promise to remain loyal to his friend came crashing down on his head, and his heart felt the indescribable sting of betraying that friend. I can only speculate what Peter might have been thinking in that moment. Perhaps, "It's all over for me now. All hope is gone. The only thing that awaits me is the disdain of my companions and the judgment of God."

When Jesus turned and looked at Peter, he saw an angry and defiant man, a man whose adamant declarations of undying allegiance had withered at the sound of a servant girl's voice. But what did Peter see when he looked at Jesus? Into what kind of eyes did he gaze? On what kind of face did he look?

Was it the face of a well-groomed yuppie? Was it the face of a freshly washed, neatly manicured businessman? Was it the face of a nicely shaved, nattily attired politician? Hardly. I'll tell you what Peter saw. He looked into blackened eyes, virtually closed from the savage beating Jesus had endured. Bruised cheeks, swollen jaw, bloodied nose, with the vile and venomous spittle of his mockers dripping from his beard.

Peter looked with horror at the face of Jesus, barely recognizable. And what look did Jesus give Peter? The face can create all sorts of looks. Our eyes alone can communicate virtually every human emotion. There is the sexually charged, flirtatious look that passes between two teenagers in the hallway at school. There is the intimidating stare of two boxers in the middle of the ring. There are the "looks that kill" and the looks that pass between two people after one has abandoned and betrayed the other. There is the I-told-you-so look, that unmistakable facial contortion reminding one of past failures and broken promises—it is a condescending glare, a look of smug superiority. The look of anger is one we all know well. No words are necessary, only a disdainful sneer that says, "Some friend you turned out to be! Where were you when I needed you most?" We've all been on the receiving (and sending) end of the look of resentment. I'm talking about one of those after-all-I've-done-for-you-this-is-what-I-get-in-return looks. Perhaps the most painful look of all is the one of disappointment. Combined with a sad shaking of the head it says, "You sorry, no-good bum. I should have expected something like this from someone like you."

Perhaps at this stage each of us needs to ask ourselves, How does Jesus look at me when I fail him, deny him, and turn my back on him? But more to the point, how did Jesus look at Peter? Was it with disdain or disappointment or anger or resentment? I don't think so. I wasn't there; I can only speculate. Neither Matthew nor Mark nor Luke nor John tells us. But knowing Jesus as I do and seeing Peter's response, I think I have a pretty good idea.

I think Jesus turned toward Peter with a look that he recognized immediately, a look of incredible power, enough to bring down the stone barriers of a military fortress. In this case, it pierced the sinful walls of Peter's stricken heart. It was the same look Peter had seen Jesus give so many times before—to Zacchaeus, the woman at the well, the woman taken in adultery. Many lepers and prostitutes and tax-collectors had been the focus of those penetrating eyes of love, hope, and forgiveness. And then Peter remembered, and he went outside and wept bitterly.

So what did Peter see in those bruised and bloodied eyes? There were no words uttered, but the eyes of Jesus spoke loudly and clearly something like, "It's OK Peter. I know your heart. I know that deep down inside you really do love me. I know the brokenness and devastation you feel right now. It really is OK. I still love you as much now as I ever did before. It's OK. It's really OK." That is how steadfast love responds even in the face of our sinful, fearful, self-protective denials of who Jesus is.

It was more than Peter could believe. After what he'd done, knowing what he deserved, the eyes of Jesus said that there's still hope; his love for him is as steadfast and certain as it has always been.

This isn't to say that Jesus didn't wince upon hearing Peter's denials. What Jesus felt may have been just like the pain you and I feel when we're abandoned by those we counted on. Our trust in others is betrayed. We find ourselves all alone, with nothing but the echo of empty promises and unfulfilled pledges. When we've needed someone most, we hear only their words of rejection. In place of a friend, we get a foe; instead of a companion, we find a coward. What kind of look do we communicate to those who treat us, in our hour of need, like Peter treated Jesus in his?

Paul twice wrote that you must forgive one another "as God in Christ forgave you" (Eph. 4:32; Col. 3:13). If you ever find yourself wondering how to do this, think of Peter's lapse. Then think of Jesus's look. That's how.

But this is not the end of the story for Peter. I said earlier that there were two events that reveal to us the depths of God's steadfast love and the forgiveness and the possibility for hope and restoration that he brings. We've seen the first in Jesus's remarkable look of love. What is the second?

I could be wrong, but I don't think this look of loving forgiveness was in itself enough to get Peter over the hump and back in the game, so to speak. It helped. Peter's broken heart was led to life-giving repentance. But something more needed to occur.

Peter was probably still filled with self-doubt and anxiety, feeling disqualified as an apostle. I can almost hear him say, "Even if I'm forgiven, I can't believe Jesus would ever want to see me again. Even if he did, I'm probably forever disqualified from ministry. Better for everyone that I just slip away into the shadows."

But Jesus wasn't yet done with Peter. Mark 16:1–8 tells us what happened on resurrection Sunday after the Sabbath. Mary Magdalene, Mary the mother of James, and Salome brought spices so that they could anoint Jesus's body. When they arrived at the tomb, they were stunned to see the stone rolled away and an angel dressed in a white robe. Here are his words to them: "Do not be alarmed. You seek Jesus of Nazareth, who was crucified. He has risen; he is not here. See the place where they laid him. But go, tell his disciples *and Peter* that he is going before you to Galilee. There you will see him, just as he told you" (Mark 16:6–7).

It's not unreasonable to believe that the risen Christ gave explicit instructions to that angel, something like, "Now listen carefully. When you tell the women to report back to the disciples that I'll meet them in Galilee, be absolutely certain you mention Peter by name. Single him out. Make a point of him so those women will know without a doubt that he is included."

I wish I had been present to see the women rush into the room where the disciples had gathered. Out of breath, overcome by joy and indescribable excitement, they speak the words that none of the disciples ever expected to hear: "He has risen! The angel said to go to Galilee and Jesus would meet all of you there" (see Mark 16:7). At this point, I can almost imagine Peter, sitting in the corner, hiding in the shadows, hoping no one would notice his presence and saying to himself, "Well, that's great. He's alive. But there's no way I'm going to Galilee. I can't bear the thought of looking into his face again. Worse still, he probably can't bear the thought of looking at me."

"Oh, yeah. Peter!" shouted Mary and Salome, "he mentioned you specifically. I'm not sure why, but that angel made a point of using your name. He singled you out. You're included. You're supposed to come too. Jesus wants to see you."

Unless I miss my guess, that was when steadfast love and forgiveness became more than just words for Peter. The reality of restoration, hope, cleansing, and a fresh start came flooding into his soul, wave upon wave of joy, gratitude, and delight. And now it's time for us to recall Paul's exhortation to us all: "Be kind to one another, tenderhearted, forgiving one another, as God in Christ forgave you" (Eph. 4:32). Precisely how and to what extent has God forgiven us? Ask Peter.

Conclusion

Let me close this chapter with a word of encouragement. I strongly suspect that many of you, maybe even most, believe that you have so horribly failed in your Christian life that you tremble at the thought of looking Jesus in the eye. It may not be as bad as Peter's denial of him. For some of you, it may be something even worse. But here is the only thing that matters: He still loves you. He's still for you. He's still here with you and has promised never, ever to leave you or forsake you.

Perhaps you live in fear of the second coming of Jesus. Perhaps the prospect of looking at him, or even more so, the prospect of him looking at you, is terrifying. But I can assure you of this. Because of who he is, his steadfast love, his unchanging character, the unbreakable promises he has made to you, his atoning death in your place, and his bodily resurrection, when he looks you in the face you will see the look of love, forgiveness, grace, and kindness. I'm absolutely certain that you will see what Peter saw: a look of undying, never-ending, heartfelt, and steadfast love and joy. Be encouraged Christian friend!

5

The Touch of Steadfast Love

IN THE PREVIOUS CHAPTER we examined what I referred to as the look of steadfast love, that piercing glance from Jesus to Peter that displayed for us the depths of our Lord's affection. In this chapter I want to explore what I'm calling the touch of steadfast love, which further shows us how such care extends not only to the soul but also the body, not just personal guilt but social shame.

The story is told both in Matthew 8:1–4 and in Mark 1:40–45. We'll focus our attention on the former. There we read,

> When he came down from the mountain, great crowds followed him. And behold, a leper came to him and knelt before him, saying, "Lord, if you will, you can make me clean." And Jesus stretched out his hand and touched him, saying, "I will; be clean." And immediately his leprosy was cleansed. And Jesus said to him, "See that you say nothing to anyone, but go, show yourself to the priest and offer the gift that Moses commanded, for a proof to them."

Leprosy

Leprosy is something that few of us have seen, and I'm sure we'd like to keep it that way. It is not an enjoyable subject that we might discuss around the dinner table. But discuss it we must. If we are to grasp the extent of our Lord's steadfast love for sinners like you and me, we need to explore both the physical and religious implications of this horrid disease.

Although there were different forms of leprosy in the ancient world, most scholars believe that the man in Matthew 8 suffered from one of the more disfiguring and contagious kinds known as lepromatous. Leprosy of this sort would begin with the discoloration of a patch of skin that would soon spread rapidly in all directions. Spongy tumors would swell up on the face and body, rendering the victim unsightly to all. The skin around the eyes and ears would begin to bunch up, with deep furrows between the swellings. Then, the tissues between the bones of the hands and feet would deteriorate, leaving fingers and toes badly deformed. It wasn't uncommon in those days for one's digits to quite literally fall off. The disease often attacked the larynx as well, giving the voice a rasping, grating sound. The odor of a leper was unmistakable and highly offensive.

Further, modern research has shown us that this disease (now called Hansen's disease) has a strange cruelty in that it often acts as an anesthetic, numbing the pain cells of hands, feet, eyes, and ears. Doctor Paul Brand, an expert on leprosy has worked with thousands of cases. He describes instances of leprosy that graphically illustrate the effect this affliction has on a person's body. For example, he witnessed one incident in which a man "reached directly into a charcoal fire to retrieve a dropped potato," never feeling any pain from the fire.[1] According to one report, "patients at Brand's hospital in India would work all day gripping a shovel with a protruding nail, or extinguish a burning wick with their bare hands, or walk on splintered glass."[2] If an ankle turned, tearing tendon and muscle, he would adjust and walk crooked. In yet another case, a man went blind because of leprosy. Each day "he would wash his face with a hot washcloth. But neither his hands nor his face was sensitive enough to temperature to warn him that he was using scalding water. Gradually he destroyed both eyes with his daily washing."[3]

But there was something else about leprosy that made it unlike all other diseases in the ancient world. It had to do less with the physical symptoms of the affliction and more with its social consequences and religious message.

The Jews abhorred leprosy and were repulsed by it not simply because of the illness itself but because it rendered the victim religiously defiled and ceremonially unclean. Leprosy, more so than any other disease, was interpreted as a curse imposed by God. There were over sixty different ways in the Mosaic Law that contact would render a person defiled. Touching a leper was second only to the defilement incurred by touching a dead body. We read this in Leviticus: "The leprous person who has the disease shall wear torn clothes and let the hair of his head hang loose, and he shall cover his upper lip and cry out, 'Unclean, unclean.' He shall remain unclean as long as he has the disease. He is unclean. He shall live alone. His dwelling shall be outside the camp" (Lev. 13:45–46).

---

1   Philip Yancey, *Where Is God When It Hurts?* (Grand Rapids, MI: Zondervan, 1990), 40.
2   Yancey, *Where Is God?*, 40.
3   Yancey, *Where Is God?*, 43.

Why was a leper required to behave in this manner? The reason is that, in the minds of the Israelites, leprosy was a form of living death (see Num. 12:12). During Jesus's day lepers were allowed to attend a synagogue but were isolated or quarantined in a booth or chamber set off to the side. In the Middle Ages, if a man contracted leprosy, the priest would lead him into the church and read the burial service over him. For all practical purposes, he was dead.

Leviticus 13:46 thus tells us that the leper was forced to live alone, away from the community and his family. The Israelites knew that God created men and women to live in society, in fellowship with others, and that God dwelled in the camp, so to live outside the camp was to be cut off from the covenant, cut off from the divine presence, cut off from the blessings of God. Being compelled to live outside the camp was one of the more egregious forms of punishment, short only of execution. It signaled not simply removal from society but removal from God.

Overall, a leper was, quite literally, cut off from his people. One Jewish rabbi is reported to have said that he would not even eat an egg that had been purchased on a street where a leper passed by. At least during biblical times, no disease so radically separated a person from his fellow man as did leprosy. This was not just because leprosy was a highly contagious disease but even more so because leprosy symbolized the devastating and disfiguring presence of sin. It is as if God selected one sickness out of the many to demonstrate the meaning of evil and its tragic effects on individuals and society at large. Just as sin separates us from God and one another, so too does leprosy. It disfigures and eats away at one's body much in the way that sin does to one's soul. We know that sin and idolatry can paralyze our hearts and render us insensitive to God and to others; leprosy has much the same effect. Sin leads to isolation and ultimately to death; leprosy does too.

But please don't misunderstand what I'm saying. I'm not suggesting that lepers were more sinful than anyone else or that they lacked dignity. Lepers were created in the image of God just like you and me. It was the disease itself, not the victim, that symbolized the damaging effects of sin. This helps us understand the unusual choice of terms to describe what happened when a leper was delivered from his disease. Whenever Jesus ministered to a leper he is said to have cleansed them of their disease rather than merely to have healed them. There is only one exception to this, and it is found in Luke 17:15 where the leper was a Samaritan, not a Jew. Consider the instructions Jesus gave to his apostles: "Heal the sick, raise the dead, cleanse lepers, cast out demons" (Matt. 10:8). Simply put, leprosy symbolized spiritual defilement. The leper's physical condition represented our spiritual state of being. We are all, in a very real sense, spiritual lepers in need of cleansing from the disfiguring stain of our sin.

Now, you may wonder why I've gone into such graphic detail to describe this man's condition. As unpleasant as it was, it was necessary to highlight the incomprehensibly merciful and loving mindset of Jesus. But first let's look more closely at this man who approached Jesus.

The first thing that speaks to me is his courage and boldness. The mere fact that he came to Jesus is remarkable in itself. Lepers were accustomed to running away from the general populace, not coming to them. This man knew he was required by law to stand aloof and apart from non-lepers. He knew he risked being stoned should he dare to draw near. Don't overlook the fact that Matthew 8:1 says "great crowds" were following Jesus. One can't help but wonder how this leper even managed to get close to our Lord. He would undoubtedly have shouted "Unclean! Unclean!" as a warning to all who were present to leave the area as quickly as they could. Some lepers even wore bells, signaling their approach. The crowd would have been alerted to his arrival and split apart, making way for this man to approach Jesus. People would have scattered in every direction to get out of the leper's way and let him through. Everyone except Jesus.

Why was this leper so bold? Why would he risk being stoned to get to our Lord? Perhaps he saw something in Jesus that he had never seen in anyone else. Perhaps he sensed a tenderness and compassion and concern that no one else had ever shown him. Perhaps he knew he was in the presence of steadfast love! Somehow he could see that Jesus was neither afraid of him nor repulsed by him. He sensed that Jesus, unlike everyone else, was not ashamed to associate with him. In some way or other, this leper saw embodied in Jesus the sort of steadfast love for people like him that he had never encountered before.

We should also take note of his reverence. Matthew says that he "knelt" down before Jesus and called him "Lord" (8:2). Kneeling in this way was often an act of worship, although "Lord" was sometimes used as the equivalent of "sir" with little to no religious implications. However, when these two things are combined, it strongly suggests more than polite deference, more than public courtesy. This conclusion is reinforced by what he says next: "Lord, if you will, you can make me clean" (8:2).

Faith never demands anything of God as a right, as if we are entitled to any of his blessings. Faith is bold, but it always submits to the sovereign purpose and timing of God. This man left himself in the hands of Jesus to be dealt with as Jesus desired. I find it in-

structive that Jesus didn't rebuke him for his use of the word "if,"
as if this were an indication of the leper's lack of a robust faith. It
saddens me to have to say this, but I fear that when some say to
God, "Heal!" they are in effect saying, "Heel!" as if God is subject
to their command and must obey their every word and wish. But
God will not be domesticated. He loves us with a steadfast love,
but his will is always supreme in how that love is expressed. He is
not our slave. We must never think that by using some formula or
having enough faith God must respond to our wishes.

Thus, although this leper refused to assume that Jesus wanted
to heal him, he was entirely confident that Jesus could do this if
he wanted to. He said, "If you will, you *can* make me clean" (v. 2).
There were no doubts in his mind about the ability of Christ to
cleanse him of this horrid affliction. Evidently this confession of
confidence in Christ's power pleased our Lord enough that he
responded, "I will; be clean" (v. 2).

The Power of a Touch

People present that day would have expected Jesus to conform to
the legal, religious, and customary requirements of dealing with a
leper. Jewish tradition prohibited anyone from coming closer than
six feet to a leper. If you were standing downwind from a leper, you
had to remain at least 150 feet away! What you must understand
is that no one, literally no one, was ever supposed to touch a leper.
And probably no one wanted to—except Jesus.

Jesus by no means had to touch him. He could have waved his
hand in the man's direction or simply spoken the words "Be healed."
It would have been no problem or drain on his power for Jesus to
cleanse the man from a distance, as he had on other occasions. In
fact, in the paragraph that follows in Matthew 8, Jesus heals the

servant of a centurion without seeing him or making any physical contact (Matt. 8:5–13; see John 4:46–54). So why did Jesus touch the leper? In Mark's account of this story, we read that Jesus was "moved with pity" (or compassion) and "stretched out his hand and touched him" (Mark 1:41). Both Matthew and Mark could as easily have said Jesus was motivated by his love for this man, steadfast love no less.

I love the physical intimacy found in Christian community. I enjoy entering a church service or a small group gathering where believers shake hands, hug one another, and express their love in other tangible ways. Paul encouraged believers to "greet one another with a holy kiss" (Rom. 16:16; see 1 Cor. 16:20; 2 Cor. 13:12; 1 Thess. 5:26).

Think about our leper. He was undoubtedly quite desperate for human touch. Ever since he contracted the disease he had been cut off from all physical contact. In Luke's account of this story, he says this man was "full of leprosy" (Luke 5:12), indicating that the disease was in an advanced stage and that the man had been suffering for years. Years without ever knowing the joy of being touched by someone else. Years without ever feeling any form of physical contact. Years of falling asleep at night entirely alone, no doubt aching for even another leper to touch him.

I struggle to find words to describe what this man must have felt when Jesus extended his hand and touched him. He may have initially recoiled, stepping back from Jesus out of fear that making contact with him would render Jesus ceremonially unclean. He probably looked around and saw the crowds standing back, literally holding their noses, covering their eyes, turning their backs—everyone, that is, except for Jesus. Ignoring the six-foot barrier, Jesus calmly walked over and touched him.

There's one more factor in this story that we should note. Matthew tells us that this incident took place when Jesus "came down from the mountain" (Matt. 8:1). Why is that significant? Simply because the mountain Jesus just descended from was the place where he had only moments before delivered the Sermon on the Mount (Matt. 5–8). He had to have been exhausted. I know how I feel after preaching. I'm tired and worn out, and the last thing I want is to be surrounded by "great crowds" pressing in and asking questions or making demands. But here is Jesus, descending from the lofty heights of the most famous public discourse ever delivered into the depths of the dark world of a leper, a social and spiritual outcast, and doing what no one else on the face of the earth would ever dare to do. He would not slip away into the greenroom set aside for the comfort and refreshment of guest speakers. He was unafraid to mingle with the crowds and wasn't in the least resentful of the demands they placed on him.

I wish I had been present to witness the transformation in this man's body. Tumors suddenly disappeared. All swelling subsided. Every disfigurement in his flesh gone in an instant. His skin, now smooth and supple.

The good news of the kingdom is very much about the steadfast love of our Lord. It is seen in his sinless life, sacrificial and substitutionary death on the cross, and bodily resurrection. But it also includes the power of the Holy Spirit in Jesus healing the sick, cleansing the lepers, and restoring hope to otherwise hopeless people. The gospel reminds us that no one need ever feel too unclean to come to Christ. No one is too sinful, too leprous, to be excluded.

Most of those who stood watching that day would have assumed that by touching a leper, Jesus would have been rendered unclean.

But no—in being touched by Jesus, this leper is made clean. As D. A. Carson has said, "When Jesus comes in contact with defilement, he is never defiled. Far from it: his touch has the power to cleanse defilement."[4]

So why did Jesus discourage the man from telling others of his healing? Perhaps he wanted to avoid people thinking of him primarily as a wonder-worker, as if his ministry was little more than a magic show. Unfortunately, the man disobeyed. Mark records it for us: "But he went out and began to talk freely about it, and to spread the news, so that Jesus could no longer openly enter a town, but was out in desolate places, and people were coming to him from every quarter" (Mark 1:45). I can't justify this man's disobedience to what Jesus asked of him, but I can understand how his joy and newfound freedom were too wonderful to not proclaim to others.

Conclusion

Like Jesus's forgiveness of Peter, his healing of the leper shows us the steadfast love of God for soiled and shame-filled men and women like you and me. Perhaps it is bodily defilement from sexual infidelity or addiction to pornography, alcohol, or drugs that makes you feel unclean and fearful of drawing near to Jesus. Maybe you've socially shamed yourself through slander, gossip, theft, or abuse. But if you come in faith, as the leper did in our story, the steadfast love of the Lord will set you free and restore hope for the days ahead. Whether it is the look that Peter beheld in the face of Jesus or the sensation of a physical touch from someone communicating the love of Christ, perhaps for the first time in years, the steadfast love of the Lord never ceases. It is new every morning.

---

4   D. A. Carson, *When Jesus Confronts the World: An Exposition of Matthew 8-10* (Grand Rapids, MI: Baker, 1987), 20.

6

Strengthened by the Spirit
to Enjoy God's Love

"HOUSTON, WE'VE HAD A PROBLEM!"[1] It's been over fifty years
since those ominous words were spoken by the astronauts on board
Apollo 13. But they are forever etched in our memory and are often
repeated by others when a threat of some substance stands in their
way. So, let me join the chorus of voices and say quite unequivo-
cally, "Houston, we have a problem!"

Or perhaps I should say, "God, we have a problem!" The problem
is simply this: you may have read the previous chapters about the
variety of ways in which God's steadfast love is the only lasting answer and solution to the many problems we face daily and yet fail to
experience that love in a personally transformative way. It is entirely
possible to memorize those scriptures, recite them with precision,
embroider them, hang them on the wall of your living room, and
yet never feel the intensity of God's affection for you, his child.

---

1 "50 Years Ago: Houston, We've Had a Problem," NASA, April 13, 2020, https://www
.nasa.gov/.

I'm not in any way minimizing the importance of meditating on Scripture or memorizing it. We should immerse our souls in the affirmations of God's steadfast love and sing loudly of the countless ways that it's our only hope. But many do this and continue to experience a disconnect between what they say and sing on the one hand and their capacity to feel God's love and be changed by it on the other.

It is even possible for someone like me to write a book about God's steadfast love and yet never be the recipient of its sin-killing, life-changing impact. I might succeed in defining God's love and providing you with evocative illustrations of what it is like and yet fail to truly comprehend what it tells me about God and his commitment to me in Christ Jesus. We can read the biblical texts, define our terms, listen to sermons on the subject, and yet fail to actually enter into the depths of experiencing the truth of God's love and the joy that we've been told will come in its wake.

The problem is that without the Holy Spirit igniting a fire in our hearts and disclosing to us the immeasurable dimensions of God's steadfast love, we will remain hopelessly dead in the water, disappointed and perhaps even disillusioned by the fact that the truth of God's word has not made the slightest difference in our relationship with him. The bottom line is that we need help, the sovereign, supernatural help of the Holy Spirit, to energize our souls to believe what we just saw in John 13 and in our Lord's response to Peter on the night he betrayed him.

There are several biblical texts that speak directly to this problem, but before we dive deeply into one of them, I want to think carefully about what it means to experience God's love and share a bit of my own personal journey regarding the experiential dimension of

Christian living. My hope is that you may find something to identify with and be encouraged by in your own pilgrimage with God.

Experiencing the Truth

First, let's be careful that we don't draw any unwarranted conclusions from distinguishing between the theological and experiential. If something you or I experience isn't theologically true—that is to say, if it isn't warranted and grounded by the clear teaching of the Bible or happens to be in direct conflict with what is in the Bible—it is a bad experience (perhaps even a misleading or destructive one).

Countless people, some of whom you undoubtedly know, have reported experiencing something in their relationship with God that, on closer inspection, has no basis in the Bible. No one is questioning whether they had an experience. It may well be a life-changing experience. It may well be a deeply religious and spiritual experience. But if the experience itself is contrary to what the Bible says, it is useless. Worse still, it is dangerous.

What I want to share with you now is my experience of biblical truth. Biblical truth isn't something only to be believed. Believe it we must! But much biblical truth is also something that God wants us to experience—to feel, sense, and enjoy. And one glorious truth that all of us should experience in the depths of our hearts but often fail to is God's love for us.

That God loves us is a fact. It is an undeniable, unshakable, unalterable fact that was demonstrated preeminently in the death of Jesus Christ. For example, we read this in Romans 5:6: "But God shows his love for us in that while we were still sinners, Christ died for us" (Rom. 5:8; see Gal. 2:20). Listen to the words of the apostle John: "In this the love of God was made manifest among us, that God sent his only Son into the world, so that we might live through him. In this is love, not that we have loved God but that he loved us and sent his Son to be the propitiation for our sins" (1 John 4:9–10).

In other words, God "shows," "manifests," or "demonstrates" his love by sending his Son, Jesus Christ, to die in our place and satisfy God's wrath against us. That is the heart of the Christian gospel. But God doesn't intend for it to stop there. The demonstration of his love is something he also intends for us to experience, enjoy, and feel deep within.

Now listen carefully. I'm not putting experience ahead of fact. I'm not saying that experience is more important than fact. I'm simply saying that this fact of God's love for us is something he wants us to feel in the depths of our inner being.

Sadly, there are a lot of people who feel loved by God but, in reality, are not. We read in John 3:36, "Whoever believes in the Son has eternal life; whoever does not obey the Son shall not see life, but the wrath of God remains on him." A lot of people are persuaded that they are the children of God and will spend eternity in heaven when they die. But these same people do not believe and obey Christ or accept his gospel as set forth in Scripture. They are not God's children. They are, as Jesus said of the Pharisees of his day, the children of the devil—"You are of your father the devil, and your will is to do your father's desires" (John 8:44). My point is simply this: Unless your trust and hope and belief are in Jesus Christ as the incarnate Son of God who died in your place on the cross, that feeling you experience of being loved by God is a lie. You are deceived. Your experience notwithstanding, the wrath of God remains on you.

So merely having an experience of being loved by God doesn't count for anything if the God who you believe loves you isn't the

God of the Bible. And if your religious encounter with the love of Jesus Christ isn't rooted in the historical reality of the incarnation, substitutionary death, and bodily resurrection of the Jesus of the Bible, that experience doesn't count either. In fact, it's worse than nothing because it actually keeps you from pursuing and knowing the true love of the true God in the truth of who Jesus Christ is and what he has done for sinners.

But having a true experience of God's love is what being a Christian is all about. That kind of experience is what I want to talk about now.

My Personal Journey

Although I have been a Christian since I was nine years old, it wasn't until I was in my late thirties that I realized that this truth was designed to be more than a known fact, more than a theological confession; it was also designed to be a felt reality or sensible experience. My own encounter with the passionate affection and undying delight that God has for me first came when I discovered Zephaniah 3:17. There we read that "the LORD your God is in your midst, a mighty one who will save; he will rejoice over you with gladness; he will quiet you by his love; he will exult over you with loud singing." Close on the heels of Zephaniah 3:17 was the prayer of Paul in Ephesians 3:14–21, which also deeply affected me. It reads,

> For this reason I bow my knees before the Father, from whom every family in heaven and on earth is named, that according to the riches of his glory he may grant you to be strengthened with power through his Spirit in your inner being, so that Christ may dwell in your hearts through faith—that you, being rooted and

grounded in love, may have strength to comprehend with all the saints what is the breadth and length and height and depth, and to know the love of Christ that surpasses knowledge, that you may be filled with all the fullness of God. Now to him who is able to do far more abundantly than all that we ask or think, according to the power at work within us, to him be glory in the church and in Christ Jesus throughout all generations, forever and ever. Amen.

What made Paul's prayer so life-changing for me was seeing that the single focus of his request was that God would work in our weak hearts through the power of the Holy Spirit to enable us to know, feel, enjoy, and be forever changed by the truth of God's steadfast love for us in Christ Jesus.

But merely pointing you to the truth of God's love in Ephesians 3, Zephaniah 3, or other similar declarations would be like setting before you the most exquisite feast you've ever known with every delicacy you most enjoy and failing to give you a fork and a knife. Indeed, it would be akin to telling you how great the food is but not letting you open your mouth and make use of your teeth to chew and ingest it. So let's look more closely at Ephesians 3.

I can only speak for myself when I say this, but there are times when I struggle to believe that what Jesus said here is true. There are times when I simply can't bring myself to believe that Jesus could love people like Peter and Matthew and me, and you too!

Let me put it this way: you and I need help to believe the passages we read in previous chapters, such as Jesus washing the disciples' feet in John 13:1–5. We desperately need help not just to believe it but have it take root in the depths of our hearts, awaken our affections, and change how we think, live, and make choices. A passage like this is designed to turn our value system on its head. It is designed to revolutionize how we think about what is of ultimate importance in life. John recorded what Jesus was thinking, feeling, doing, and saying so that the truth of God's love for us in and through Jesus might penetrate and soften our hard hearts, upend our value system, and fill us with a spiritual energy that would forever transform everything in our lives.

But here's the problem. We are weak. We struggle with doubt and we secretly question the truthfulness of what Jesus said and did. We are filled with anxiety and live in fear that what we see in John 13 couldn't possibly be true. "No one can love like that," we say to ourselves. "I'd like to believe that someone can; I'd like to believe that Jesus can. But my nature and experience in life up to this point tell me otherwise. Sam, if you really want me to believe this, if you really hope that my life would be forever changed by this truth, I'm going to need a lot of help."

Yes, I know. So let me say it as clearly as I can: It takes God's power to believe in God. When God says in such breathtaking terms as he did through Jesus in passages like John 13, "I love you," it takes God himself to enable us to believe him.

The help we need for these passages to make a lasting, lifelong impact on our lives won't be found in a self-help book, the wise words of a counselor or good friend, or even a really good sermon. That's not to suggest that these could never help us, but the issue at hand is of a different order. For you and me to believe and bank our lives on the truth of God's love, we need God himself to do something miraculous in our hearts. That is why we need to pause right now and ask God to help us believe that he's actually speaking the truth to us when he describes a love that, as Paul says in Ephesians 3, surpasses knowledge, a love that is so deep and profound that if anyone other than God had said it we would instinctively call them a liar.

Praying for Strength

The opening phrase in Ephesians 3:14, "for this reason," picks up on the same phrase in Ephesians 3:1, which points back to 2:19–22 and its discussion of how God has incorporated believing Gentiles into fellowship with believing Jews as the one people of God, the dwelling place of the Holy Spirit. Also included is Paul's description in 3:1–13 of his role in assembling this ethnically diversified group. It is because of what God has done in overcoming ethnic barriers and uniting his one people as one temple for the indwelling of the Spirit that Paul now prays as he does.

Paul's posture is significant. Though standing was normal among the Jews (1 Kings 8:22; Mark 11:25; Luke 18:11; see 1 Chron. 29:20; 2 Chron. 29:29; Ezra 9:5; Ps. 95:6; Dan. 6:10; Luke 22:41; Acts 7:60; 9:40; 20:36; 21:5), Paul bows his knees. Kneeling may be an expression of his intensity. For him, intercession was a struggle, a battle, a fight (see Rom. 15:30; Col. 4:2, 12). Kneeling shows that we are coming to a sovereign whom we depend on. It is also often associated with extreme passion and neediness. It reflects our desperation.

Further, in this passage, the "family" in both "heaven and on earth" (Eph. 3:15) is probably a reference not only to angels but also Christians in heaven who are organized for worship like earthly families. That our "Father" is the one who "named" them is Paul's way of declaring that he not only created them but also exercises ultimate and absolute authority over them.

In this prayer, Paul is asking God to give his readers strength. That's clear enough. But strength for what? In what way are we weak and in need of the sort of strength that only God can give? In the next verses it becomes immediately clear that our weakness is in our failure and inability to wholeheartedly believe in, feel, and rejoice in the love that God has for us in Jesus.

Strengthened by the Spirit to Believe

Overall, Paul's prayer for us to be "strengthened" is qualified in four ways. First, it is "according to the riches of his glory." Sometimes glory is God's brightness, greatness, or renown, but it also connotes power (Col. 1:11; Rom. 6:4). Thus Paul here prays that God would give his people fortitude or strength and do this out of the infinite treasures of his majestic might. That's important to remember because at various points along the way you might find yourself battling doubt as to whether God can pull it off. Can he genuinely enable me to feel and enjoy his love? Does he have sufficient resources to overcome and subdue my fearful, anxious heart? Yes!

The word translated "according to" (Eph. 3:16) points beyond the idea of source or origin to that of proportion—Paul asks for power not merely "out of" God's riches but "according to" (or in proportion to) them. He asks for power on a scale commensurate with God's riches.

Second, this power is given "through his Spirit." The Spirit is always the one who does things for us on the inside, producing qualities and characteristics that we can't produce on our own (see Rom. 15:13; 2 Tim. 1:7). Without the ever-present, effectual power of the Holy Spirit none of this would ever happen. He is the one who strengthens us. This, then, is the first answer to the problem I posed at the beginning of this chapter: if the Holy Spirit doesn't operate in and on our hearts to provide us with the strength to overcome all our objections, fears, and hesitations about whether God really loves us, we will never walk in the freedom and peace that such love is designed to empower.

Third, this strengthening occurs in "in your inner being" (Eph. 3:16). This lets us know that the sort of strength we need can never be gained by lifting weights, faithfully going to CrossFit, or doing push-ups (see 2 Cor. 4:16). The inner being is the interior life, the core of our personality, and the center of our identity. It is the person we are on the inside. Heart, mind, will, spirit, soul, and affections are all encompassed by this phrase. That's where the battle rages. That's where the enemy wants to convince us that God is lying to us about his love. That's why we are "weak" in the inner being and need to be made strong.

Fourth, the purpose or goal of this inner spiritual strengthening is that "Christ may dwell in your hearts through faith" (Eph. 3:17). The Christians in first-century Ephesus, just like you and me, were already sealed by the Spirit (1:13), united with Christ in his resurrection and exaltation (2:5–6), and incorporated into one body where the Spirit dwells (2:22). Paul will even say in Colossians 1:27 that "the hope of glory" is "Christ in you." So it can't be that Christ didn't already dwell in them or doesn't now dwell in us. What we lack is the encouragement and incentive to draw on this truth—the ability or capacity to experience it in life-changing ways.

Paul is clearly praying to God for our felt experience of the person of Christ. He prays that we might be internally strengthened by the Spirit so that Christ might dwell in our hearts. But how can that be if we had already received Christ into our hearts when we were born again? The only viable explanation is that Paul is referring to an experiential enlargement of what is already theologically true. He wants us to be strengthened by the Spirit so that Jesus might exert a progressively greater and more intense personal influence in our souls.

The result of this expansion of the divine power and presence in our hearts is the ability to "comprehend" or grasp "what is the breadth and length and height and depth" (Eph. 3:18) of Christ's love for us. Paul clearly wants his readers, and that includes all of us, to understand Christ's love. But how is this possible if this love "surpasses knowledge" (v. 18)? How can you know what can't be known? Clearly, this is not just an intellectual exercise. This is Paul's way of saying that God intends for us to feel and experience and be emotionally moved by the passionate affection he has for us, his children.

When Paul says that we need strength to experience the indwelling presence and power of Christ, he says this comes through "faith" (3:17). I think his point is that our weakness is in the area of faith: we simply don't believe what we read in Zephaniah 3 or John 3:16 or any of those incredible descriptions in the Psalms of God's steadfast love. We waver in our confidence. We worry that it might all turn out to be only a dream, perhaps a nightmare. Our faith must be strengthened and intensified. And only the Holy Spirit can make that happen!

Strengthened Together

There are two words typically used in the New Testament for the concept of indwelling. The first, *paroikeō*, means to abide or to inhabit, but not necessarily permanently. The second, used in Ephesians 3:17, is *katoikeō* which emphasizes "a settling in or colonising tenancy."[2] The verb emphasizes the idea of living permanently (see

2   Ernest Best, *A Critical and Exegetical Commentary on Ephesians* (London: T&T Clark, 1998), 341.

Col. 2:9). Christ doesn't sojourn in our hearts. He is no divine nomad. He is a permanent, abiding resident.

This indwelling influence is in some way related to being "rooted and grounded in love" (Eph. 3:17). Here Paul employs a double metaphor: one from agriculture and one from architecture. Love, according to Paul, "is the soil in which believers are to be rooted and grow, the foundation on which they are to be built."[3] Clearly, then, a precondition for experiencing the fullness of Christ's indwelling presence is having been rooted and grounded in love. But whose love? Is it God's love for us in Christ? That would mean you are rooted and grounded in God's love for you so that you can know God's love for you, which seems a bit odd. Is it our love for God? No, for that can't enable us to know his love for us. What Paul is referring to is our love for one another. In other words, this is not merely an individual experience. It happens in community, as together we live, enjoy, and grow in our ability to believe and be satisfied with God's love for us.

Here in verse 18 Paul comes full circle. He has prayed that God would strengthen us through the Spirit. We asked the question, What for? Here is the answer: we need "strength" in our inner being "to comprehend with all the saints what is the breadth and length and height and depth" of God's love. Again, note the communal emphasis on this experience—we experience God's love together "with" all the other believers in our local church. For all its glory and the great heights from which it came, such love can only be experienced "together with all the saints" (see 1:1, 15; 6:18)! Thus our experience of Christ's love is personal but not private. It is meant to be felt and proclaimed and enjoyed in the

---

3 Andrew T. Lincoln, *Ephesians*, Word Biblical Commentary (Dallas: Word Books, 1990), 207.

context of the body of Christ. This is no isolated, individualistic, esoteric experience "but the shared insight gained from belonging to the community of believers."[4]

Strengthened beyond Measure

But how are we to measure such love? What are its dimensions? Does it come in meters or miles? Do we measure it in yards or pounds? Does Paul intend for you to think in terms of mathematical proportions, as if to suggest that God loves you a hundred times more than he loves the angels or fifty times less than he loves a godlier Christian?

Quite the contrary, says Paul. There is a width, length, height, and depth to Christ's love for you, but it goes beyond human measurement. Its immensity and magnitude is incalculable. Its dimensions defy containment. It is beyond knowing. You can't compare it to the height of Mount Everest or the distance between earth and the most distant galaxy. The deepest part of the ocean is a mere fraction of the depths of God's steadfast love for his people. It is infinitely broader than the chasm of the Grand Canyon and indescribably longer than any trip that a spaceship could undertake. Yet Paul prays that we might know it! This deliberate oxymoron (a statement of apparent inconsistency) serves to deepen what is already too deep to fathom.

Thus verse 19—to "know the love of Christ that surpasses knowl-edge"—simply restates verse 18. To grasp the incalculable love of Christ for his own is to know what can't be known! This theological paradox is designed to emphasize that what we know in part is ultimately incomprehensible. We may know Christ's love in some

---

4   Lincoln, *Ephesians*, 213.

measure, but we will never exhaustively comprehend it. No matter how much we learn, no matter how much we think we know and see and feel and grasp, there is always an infinity left over! Thus, God's love for us in Christ is so vast and immense and immeasurable that it takes God himself strengthening us through the indwelling Christ to make sense of it.

The ultimate result is that you and I might "be filled with all the fullness of God," (3:19) meaning his moral perfections or excellencies as well as his empowering presence, or all that God is as God. But with what are we to be filled? Is it the power of God? Or perhaps it's the love of Christ? Could it be the Holy Spirit who fills us to overflowing? Certainly each of these is true, but there is more in Paul's mind: we are to be filled by God, "and presumably if they are to be filled up to the fullness of God, it is with this fullness that they are to be filled."[5] In some sense, then, it is with the radiant power and presence of God himself that we are to be filled, the measure of which is God himself. Whereas the church as Christ's body already shares in, embodies, and expresses his fullness (Eph. 1:23), we have not yet experienced the plenitude of God in the way that is available to us. That is why Paul now prays as he does.

I can only speak for myself, but this far exceeds my intellectual and spiritual capacity to grasp. I'm left breathless even now as I write these words. To think that God loves me so deeply and intensely and sacrificially that he works in me by his Spirit to make it possible for God himself to fill me up with God himself—what words can adequately account for this?

Has Paul gone too far in this prayer? Has he asked for something that not even God himself can provide? Has his boldness

5   Lincoln, *Ephesians*, 214.

gotten out of hand? No, and verses 20–21 tell us why. Paul writes, "Now to him who is able to do far more abundantly than all that we ask or think, according to the power at work within us, to him be glory in the church and in Christ Jesus throughout all generations, forever and ever. Amen." Here, Paul's effusive praise of God reflects the unbounded bounty of his ability to bless his people in response to their prayers. According to the apostle, God is able to *do* (or to work), for he is neither idle nor inactive, nor dead (contrast the dumb idols in Ps. 115:1–8). He is able to do what we *ask*, for he hears and answers the very prayers that he commands we pray. When it is God's will to bestow a blessing, he graciously incites the human heart to ask for it. He is able to do what we ask or *think*, for he reads our thoughts, and sometimes we imagine things that we are afraid to articulate and therefore do not ask. In other words, his ability to provide for us must never be measured by the limits of our spoken requests. He is able to do *all* that we ask or think (not just some of it), for he knows it all and can perform it all. There is nothing that is proper for us to have that transcends or outstrips his power to perform. He is able to do *more than* all that we ask or think, for his power infinitely exceeds our most expansive requests. He is able to do *more abundantly* than all that we ask or think, for he does not give his grace by calculated measure. He is able to do very much more or *far more abundantly* than all that we ask or think, for he is a God of superabundance (the Greek word here has the idea of an extraordinary degree or considerable excess beyond expectations). All that he does is by virtue of his power that even now energetically works within us. This is the same power that raised Jesus from the dead and seated him in the heavenlies above all principalities and powers (see Eph. 1:19–23).

So, yes, we have a problem. But it is one that is wonderfully solved by the power of the Holy Spirit silencing our objections, overcoming our anxieties, and filling us with the undeniable awareness of the magnitude of God's steadfast love.

7

Love in the Most Famous
Verse in the Bible

JOHN 3:16 MAY WELL BE the most famous verse in the entire Bible. Even if it isn't, its truth warrants continual celebration and gratitude, especially as it relates to the theme of God's steadfast love and the way this love was demonstrated in the gift of his Son. It reads, "For God so loved the world, that he gave his only Son, that whoever believes in him should not perish but have eternal life."

God's love is foundational to everything we read in this glorious verse of Scripture. But can anything more be said about the love of God that Christians don't already know? As a matter of fact, yes!

Different Ways that God Loves

Perhaps the first thing I would point out is that God's love is not uniform or monolithic—that is to say, God loves different people and different things differently. His love is multifaceted and more complex than most people realize. That may surprise you, but consider this: God loves himself, his creation, the nation of Israel, and the elect in different ways.[1]

First, the Bible talks often of God's love for his Son, our Lord Jesus Christ, and of the Son's love for the Father. We read in John 3:35 that "the Father loves the Son and has given all things into his hand." In John 14:31, Jesus says, "I do as the Father has commanded me, so that the world may know that I love the Father." Again, in John 17:26, Jesus says he will make known the name of the Father so "that the love with which you have loved me may be in them and I in them."

This is a dimension of divine love that is almost beyond comprehension. God loves us in spite of our sin, but there is no sin in the Godhead that might impede or limit the love that the Father, Son, and Holy Spirit have for each other. There is no obstacle in the way that might diminish the love that the persons of the Godhead have for each other. Their mutual love is perfect, perpetual, and pure.

Second, there is God's love for his creation, including sinners. The psalmist declares that "the LORD is good to all, and his mercy is over all that he has made" (Ps. 145:9). And Jesus, in Matthew 5:44–45, commands us to love our enemies and pray for those who persecute us so that we may be seen to be sons of our Father who is in heaven, "for he makes his sun rise on the evil and on the good, and sends rain on the just and the unjust." God's love leads him to make gracious provision even for those who hate him.

Third, there is God's love for the nation Israel. We read of this in Deuteronomy 7:

---

1 See D. A. Carson's *The Difficult Doctrine of the Love of God* (Wheaton, IL: Crossway, 2000).

The Lord your God has chosen you to be a people for his treasured possession, out of all the peoples who are on the face of the earth. It was not because you were more in number than any other people that the Lord set his love on you and chose you, for you were the fewest of all peoples, but it is because the Lord loves you (Deut. 7:6–8).

We read about this yet again in Deuteronomy 10:14–15: "Behold, to the Lord your God belong heaven and the heaven of heavens, the earth with all that is in it. Yet the Lord set his heart in love on your fathers and chose their offspring after them, you above all peoples, as you are this day." Neither of these texts means that everyone who was an Israelite was saved. We know that many within the nation were rebellious, hard-hearted, and turned continually to idolatry. But God loved the nation as his covenant people and blessed them with countless privileges and promises. This doesn't mean there is no sense in which God loved other nations. But he didn't love them in the same way that he chose to love Israel.

Fourth, there is God's love for his elect, redeemed people. This is a love that goes beyond providing earthly blessings for them and leads to a saving relationship with him. When God loves people in this way, he is not only offering eternal life but also working in their hearts to overcome their rebellion and unbelief and leading them to faith in Jesus. This is what Paul had in mind in Ephesians 1:4–5. There he said that "in love he [God] predestined us for adoption to himself as sons through Jesus Christ, according to the purpose of his will." Again, in Ephesians 2:4–5 he said, "God, being rich in mercy, because of the great love with which he loved us, even when we were dead in our trespasses, made us alive together with Christ." This love is "great" because it actually leads God to make us alive in faith and trust and joy in Jesus. This love conquers and overcomes spiritual death and gives new and eternal life. A love that is anything less than "great" could never do this.

God Loved the World

In John 3:16, the apostle uses one word—"world" (*kosmos*)—to describe the object of God's love.[2] Many try to magnify God's love by pointing out how many people have lived in this world. "Just think," they say, "of the multitudes of men and women who have swarmed across the face of the earth. Oh, how great the love of God must be that it could encompass such a countless multitude!"

But I'm not so sure that is what John is saying here. I don't think we learn everything about God's love by counting heads. God's love is not as magnified when we ask, "How many?" as it is when we ask, "What kind?" In other words, John isn't referring to quantity but quality. In this scripture, the nature of the people whom God loves is crucial, not their number.

In other words, what makes the love of God so marvelous is that he loved, of all things, the world! The contrast here is moral, not mathematical. The difference between God and the world isn't that God is one and the world is many. The difference is that God is holy, and the world isn't. That's what makes his love so astounding. The lover is righteous and the loved are not. God therefore loved the moral antithesis of himself—light loved darkness, holiness loved wickedness, the immeasurably pure loved the indescribably defiled. Thus the "world" here is not to be thought of in terms of its size but in terms of its sinfulness. The point is not that the

---

2   See John Murray, "The Atonement and the Free Offer of the Gospel," in *Collected Writings of John Murray* (Carlisle, PA: Banner of Truth, 1976), 78–80.

world is so big that it takes a great quantity of love to love it all. The point is that the world is so bad that it takes an amazing kind of love to love it at all.

When I first met my wife, Ann, who I've been married to for over fifty-two years, I had several things in mind about the kind of woman I was looking for. I'm sure she had an image in mind of the sort of man she wanted to marry. We both valued physical health, intellectual abilities, personality traits such as kindness and humility, and compatibility. Spiritual commitment would also have ranked extremely high. But I can assure you that neither of us said anything along the lines of, "I'm willing to marry a person who utterly despises me, who is worse than indifferent toward me. I'm hoping for someone who hates me, treats me with contempt and disdain, and who wants nothing whatsoever to do with me."

But God did. When the Father sought a bride for his Son, he set his affection and love on a people who were his enemies. He loved a world that hated him. His heart was moved toward those who felt bitter enmity for him and refused to honor him as the most honorable Being in the universe. God chose to love his enemies, "for God so loved" this fallen, corrupt, wicked world. Such was the nature of the immeasurable love with which he loved us.

God's Love Gives

When we declare our love for someone, we often have in mind a stirring of our hearts, an internal affection that is expressed in words. But that is not all that love is. And God's love shows us just that. True love is a giving love, a sacrificial love. As John declares, God so loved the world that he *gave* his only Son. Paul echoed this truth when he said that the Son of God "loved me and *gave* himself for me" (Gal. 2:20). Yet again, in seeking to illustrate the quality of love that a husband should have for his wife, Paul says that "Christ loved the church and *gave* himself up for her" (Eph. 5:25).

Let this truth sink deeply into your soul: God loved this world by giving to it the last thing it could ever deserve! "For God so loved the world that he *gave* his only Son." It's as if God the Father said to God the Son, "There is something I want you to do. This world of humanity will be populated by people who hate me. They will rebel against me. Every single one of them. They will deserve nothing from me but eternal damnation. They will deserve to perish. But I want you to go and become one of them, live the life they should have lived but didn't, and die in their place the death they should have died so that I may give eternal life to as many as will accept my offer."

The death of God the Son, Jesus Christ, is the expression of the Father's love for those who hate him. Many have greatly distorted the cross of Christ by thinking of it as the means by which the love of God is won. They envision Jesus crying out from the cross, "Oh, Father, in dying for these people I have now made them loveable." No!

Love is not something wrung from the heart of a reluctant and disinclined God by the sufferings of his Son. Jesus doesn't plead from the cross, "Oh, Father, please love them now that I have died for them." No! The cross is not the attempt by Jesus to persuade or entice the Father to love us. The cross is the express manifestation of a love that the Father already had for this lost and dying world.

But don't think for a moment that it was only the love of the Father that led to the cross of Christ. Some today have wrongly interpreted the doctrine of penal substitution as the Father coercing or compelling his innocent Son to suffer for the guilty. We hear all too often of the blasphemous assertion that penal substitutionary atonement is akin to cosmic child abuse. But nothing could be further from the truth. Jesus himself declared that he "lays down his life for the sheep" (John 10:11). His point is that it was his own love and affection for the sheep that moved him to lay down his life. It was not taken from him. His life, given up on the cross, was his to give. Again, Jesus made it clear when he said, "For this reason the Father loves me, because I lay down my life that I may take it up again. No one takes it from me, but I lay it down of my own accord. I have authority to lay it down, and I have authority to take it up again" (John 10:17–18).

The Son "gave himself" (Gal. 2:20) as much as the Father sent him. The Father sent his Son, who joyfully embraced the task because he loved those he would die for. Our great triune God is a giving God, a God who initiates at great sacrifice to himself the deepest and most profound expression of love that is possible: the giving of his Son. And the Son joyfully and freely embraces the will of his Father in yielding up his life for a world of lost, hell-deserving sinners.

God Gave His Only Son

Thus, God's immeasurable love is such that he not only feels a great affection for the fallen world but that this feeling leads to concrete, sacrificial action: he gave us his Son. Muslims consider it blasphemy to suggest that God has a son. Many Mormons happily affirm that Jesus is God's son because they argue that God the Father, who has a literal, physical body, had sexual relations with Mary, who bore him a son, Jesus. But the teaching of Scripture is that the sonship of the second person of the Trinity is an eternal relation. The Father has always been the Father of the Son and the Son has always been the Son of the Father. There has never been a time when either was neither. These familial terms highlight the intimate relationship that exists between the first and second persons of the Godhead. When God gave to us, he gave us his Son.

Let's be careful we do not rush past the incredible reality that it was God's "only Son" whom he gave for us. It was his unique, special, only Son; the Son who above all others was near and dear to his heart. This truth is the basis for what Paul would say in Romans 8:32: "He who did not spare his own Son but gave him up for us all, how will he not also with him graciously give us all things?" This may well be the most glorious assurance that God could ever give us. If he was happy and joyful in making for us the single greatest sacrifice that he could, how will he not then freely and just as happily make available every provision for our spiritual flourishing both now and in the age to come!

I can well imagine that God might be willing to sacrifice an angel. For God not to "spare" an angel makes sense. After all, there are probably millions of angels. What's the loss of one from among so many? I can even envision God not sparing an archangel like Michael, for even though he loves him, this love pales infinitely in comparison with his love for his Son. I can also see God sacrificing one of the four living creatures or one of the seraphim or cherubim from Revelation. But his own precious, most highly beloved Son? How could God choose not to "spare" his own Son? Yet that is precisely what he did, so great is his immeasurable, steadfast love for the world.

As the consummate expression of his love for this fallen, defiant world of sinners, God did not spare his own Son; he made the greatest sacrifice imaginable. We thus see the magnitude of his love when we see the precious, priceless value of the gift he gave.

Believing God's Love

Yet, the eternal life that John describes in John 3:16 does not come automatically to all people. It is not bestowed on those whose children behave themselves or on people who first straighten out their lives. Eternal life is for anyone and everyone who "believes" in this gift of God's love, namely Jesus—who he is and what he has done to save sinners.

This offer is universal and indiscriminate. It extends to all people of both genders, from every ethnic group and socioeconomic category. It extends to all manner of sinners, from the most scandalous to the seemingly saintly, from the bad to the very worst.

The truth and promise of the gospel of Jesus Christ are like spiritual honey. But how do I describe the taste of honey to someone who has no taste buds? I can break down honey into its many chemical constituents. I can describe for you its color and texture. I can even explain in intricate detail the process by which it is made. But the only way for you to enjoy the taste of the honey of eternal life is actually to taste it. So taste it! Believe in Jesus and you will find him sweet to your soul and the most satisfying person you've ever known.

In other words, believing in Jesus is more than merely agreeing in your head with the facts about Jesus. It does include that, but it goes far beyond mere intellectual assent. The demons believe true things about Jesus, but they are eternally lost (James 2:19). Believing also means savoring in the most deeply satisfying way all that God is for you in Jesus. It means you treasure the one you know. You prize him above all others. You enjoy him to the fullest degree. Believing is coming to Christ and finding him to be the only one who can satisfy the deepest and most intense longings of your heart.

This mention of the necessity of believing takes us back into John 3:14–15, which says, "As Moses lifted up the serpent in the wilderness, so must the Son of Man be lifted up, that whoever believes in him may have eternal life" (see Num. 21:4–9). We know this incident was a type or foreshadowing of the death of Jesus because Jesus himself says "as" Moses lifted up the serpent, "so" must the Son of Man be lifted up. What strikes many as odd is that if the bronze snake is portrayed as a curse, it would suggest that Jesus is being portrayed in the same way. And that is true. But listen carefully. Jesus became a curse for us. Jesus became sin for us. Paul said it in two places:

> For our sake [God] made him to be sin who knew no sin, so that in him we might become the righteousness of God. (2 Cor. 5:21)

> Christ redeemed us from the curse of the law by becoming a curse for us. (Gal. 3:13)

Thus, in becoming like the snake, Jesus was the embodiment of our sin and the embodiment of our curse. And in becoming sin and a curse for us, he took ours away. Piper explains, "Jesus, in the place of the snake, is the source of healing, the source of rescue from the poison of sin, and the wrath of God. Jesus is the source of eternal life."[3]

But this deliverance from the poison of sin and the wrath of God that it brings only comes through faith. You must believe in Jesus. When the Son of Man, Jesus, is lifted up on the cross, you

---

3 John Piper, "The Son of Man Must Be Lifted Up—Like the Serpent," April 5, 2009, https://www.desiringgod.org/.

must look to him, hanging there as the substitutionary sacrifice for your sin. You must believe in him as the one who can save you from the poisonous venom of your moral and spiritual rebellion and the wrath of God that it provokes.

Before we leave this story, let me also point out what the people of Israel were not told to do. They were not encouraged to follow some path of self-reformation. They were not instructed to incorporate themselves into the Society for the Extermination of Fiery Serpents. They were not told to pray to the serpent on the pole, nor were they commanded to buy some relic of the serpent and revere it in hopes of continued well-being. Sadly, some in Israel did precisely that, as seen in 2 Kings 18:4. There we read about the spiritual reforms instituted by Hezekiah: "He removed the high places and broke the pillars and cut down the Asherah. And he broke in pieces the bronze serpent that Moses had made, for until those days the people of Israel had made offerings to it."

The point we are to glean from this is simple: We are bitten with the poison of sin just as the Israelites were of the serpents. And just as they looked to the bronze serpent for physical healing, we are to look to Jesus in faith for spiritual healing.

According to John 3:16, believing in who Jesus is and what he has done is absolutely essential for salvation and eternal life. This emphasis on believing in John 3:16 means that not everyone will benefit from the love of God in having sent his Son. It is of benefit only for those who believe, that is, those who embrace him for who he claimed to be and who trust him for what he came to accomplish.

Rejecting God's Love

But why wouldn't everyone believe? Knowing what God is offering us in his Son, why wouldn't every person joyfully and instantly believe? The answer is given in the next verses: "And this is the judgment: the light has come into the world, and people loved the darkness rather than the light because their works were evil. For everyone who does wicked things hates the light and does not come to the light, lest his works should be exposed" (3:19–20).

People reject the light of the gospel of Jesus Christ because they love spiritual and moral darkness. They fear exposure (3:20) and shame and the light of truth. They prefer to remain in darkness "because their works are evil" (3:19). The bottom line is this: many primarily reject Christ and the gospel and Christianity not for intellectual reasons but for moral reasons. It isn't that they lack evidence or think Christianity is logically incoherent. They reject Christ because to accept him and follow him means that they must abandon their sinful ways, which they love, and because they cherish the pleasures of sin more than they fear its consequences.

John then comes straight to the point without hesitation or compromise. If you do not believe in the Son, you will "perish" (3:16). To perish is the opposite of experiencing eternal life. If you gain eternal life by believing in Jesus, you are assured by God that you will never perish.

But what does it mean to "perish"? It does not mean that you cease to exist. It means that you remain under the condemnation of God's wrath and judgment. Twice in verse 18 John describes what happens if you persist in unbelief: you are condemned. Indeed, you are "condemned already." You stand condemned. God's sentence of judgment is on unbelievers and remains there as long as they refuse to repent and believe.

Later, in John 3:36, we see this stated once again: "Whoever believes in the Son has eternal life; whoever does not obey the Son shall not see life, but the wrath of God remains on him." Unbelievers are already under condemnation and remain that way forever unless they believe. To remain under God's condemnation and judgment is to perish.

People often wonder why the sin of rejecting God and his gift of love in his Son, Jesus Christ, is so serious, indeed so serious that it merits condemnation and eternal perishing. I have learned much of the answer to this question from Jonathan Edwards and John Piper. Both of these men repeatedly point out that it is because God, Father, Son, and Holy Spirit, is the infinitely precious, infinitely worthy, and most excellent person in the universe. There is no limit to his beauty and value. Everything else in the universe is utterly dependent on him for its existence. Because he is all this, we owe him perfect obedience, love, worship, honor, respect, and adoration. Thus to ignore him, neglect him, disobey him, and refuse to believe in the offer of life that comes from him is a sin deserving of infinite and eternal punishment.

To not believe what God has revealed about himself and his Son is far more than saying, "I don't find the evidence sufficiently persuasive." To not believe is to treat God with utter disregard and contempt. It is to cast aside the greatest treasure as if it were no more than worthless gravel. It is to declare that the most beautiful of all beings is offensive to the sight. It is to make known with hostile and critical intent that the most harmonious of all musical scores is a screeching cacophony of off-key clamor.

To not believe, therefore, is far, far more than mere intellectual indifference or benign disagreement. It is self-centered, arrogant defiance of the one true God and his loving, merciful, gracious offer of eternal life in his presence. That is why it is deserving of eternal damnation.

The Gift of Eternal Life with God

But what precisely is eternal life? Does this simply mean that if we believe in Jesus we will live forever? Is he referring here only to the unending duration of our existence? No, it means far more than that, because everyone, even unbelievers, will live forever. Some will live forever in the presence of God in the new heavens and new earth while others will live forever in hell.

Thus, eternal life must be something more than simply always remaining alive. Surely there is a qualitative emphasis to these words. John is not talking so much about how long we will live but about the kind or quality of the life that we will experience forever. His point here is that God's love has made provision through the life, death, and resurrection of Jesus Christ to give those who believe an eternity of unbroken, unimaginably intimate, unfathomably satisfying fellowship with and enjoyment of God himself.

Later, in his prayer to the Father as recorded in John 17, Jesus says something truly profound: "This is eternal life, that they know you, the only true God, and Jesus Christ whom you have sent" (John 17:3). Perhaps if I told you that Jesus was about to define or describe the essence of eternal life, you would think of walking on streets of gold, ruling over celestial kingdoms, judging angels, receiving a glorified body, flying to distant galaxies, or never dying or sinning. But Jesus says it consists primarily in knowing, loving, and enjoying God!

Don't ever forget that this eternal life is not something you have to wait to inherit after you die. It is yours now, from the first moment you entrust yourself to Jesus in faith. In John 5:24 Jesus says, "Truly, truly, I say to you, whoever hears my word and believes him who sent me has eternal life. He does not come into judgment, but has passed from death to life." Notice the present possession of eternal life: not "will have" but now "has"! Yes, we who believe in Jesus must still die physically, but physical death in no way severs us from Christ or interrupts our eternal life in him (see John 11:26).

8

When God Loves the Unlovely

SOMETIMES THE REALITY of God's steadfast love for his children is better explained by a story than theological argumentation. In other words, it's one thing for me to say repeatedly throughout this book, "God loves you with a steadfast love that defies our expectations and shatters our preconceived notions of what that love truly is," but it is another thing entirely for you to see that sort of love in action, in a tangible way. Though our definitions and doctrinal observations about love are limited, the meaning of this glorious truth comes alive in fresh ways when we see it in the experience of human beings. When the steadfast love of God for broken, weak, sinful people like you and me exerts a life-changing influence on us, the proverbial light bulb suddenly shines brightly above our heads, and we say, "Oh, now I see what you mean. Now I understand what God's steadfast love is all about."

That being the case, let's look closely at two of the most beautiful and encouraging stories in the Bible that drive home, deeply into our hearts, the reality of God's affection for his people. One is found in the Old Testament and the other in the New Testament.

Redeeming an Unrepentant Prostitute

Everyone loves a love story. Whether it is the tragic tale of Romeo and Juliet or the testimony of a couple in their 90's who've been happily married for seventy years, there's something about real-life men and women and their relationship that exerts an unusual influence on our hearts. But there is one love story that is about far more than one person's commitment to another. The devotion the man in this story displayed toward his wife is designed to inform you and me about the steadfast constancy of God's love for us. You probably know it well. I'm talking about the relationship between an Old Testament prophet named Hosea and a woman named Gomer.[1]

You simply can't read the narrative of Hosea and Gomer without shock and amazement. Hosea was the last to prophesy before the northern kingdom of Israel fell to Assyria in 722 BC. He may have lived 2,700 years ago, but his idea of marriage wouldn't have differed greatly from mine. Like most other men, he wanted a wife who was faithful, pure, gentle, and loving. But he didn't get one. Hosea married a whore. Sorry, but there's no reason to tone down the language. Hosea's wife, Gomer (I've often wondered if she had a brother named Goober!), was a whore, a prostitute. She was unfaithful, ungrateful, unbelieving, and unloving. Why, then, did Hosea marry her? Because God told him to. He said, "Go, take to yourself a wife of whoredom and have children of whoredom, for the land commits great whoredom by forsaking the LORD" (Hos. 1:2).

This is not a pattern for our marriages today. This is not a story in which God says, "Go and do likewise." God singled out Hosea and told him to do something that most, if not all of us, would

---

1 This retelling of the story of Hosea and Gomer is adapted from my book *The Singing God* (Lake Mary, FL: Passio, 2013), 35–38. Used by permission.

consider outrageous. But he had a reason for this odd command. Hosea and Gomer were to illustrate the steadfast love of God for his people, Israel, and by extension and application, all of us.

Hosea was to represent God. Gomer, his wife, was to play the part of Israel. Instead of simply telling his people how sinful they were and how he was determined to love them anyway, God brought Hosea and Gomer center stage to dramatically act it out. So Hosea married a harlot. He adopted the children she had conceived because of her immoral trysts. She then bore Hosea three children whom God also used to illustrate the depth of Israel's sin.

God's Rejected Children

I'm fascinated with the reasons people give for naming their children the way they do. Some select names that they hope will instill confidence in their child. Others pick whatever is fashionable at the time. I happen to be named after my grandfather. My father once told me of a family in his hometown who named their six children Victor, Vada, Vida, Velda, Vester, and Vernon! A friend of mine, less concerned with alliteration, opted for biblical names for his seven kids.

When God named the offspring of Hosea and Gomer, his decision was shaped by the lesson he wanted to teach Israel. Thus, the firstborn, a son, was named Jezreel, which meant "God scatters." This clearly pointed to the judgment that would befall Israel. The second child was a daughter, Lo-Ruhamah, which meant "not pitied." And the third child, another son, was called Lo-Ammi, "not my people." I have honestly felt sorry for these kids. Can you imagine the taunting and ridicule they endured from their peers while growing up? I've often wondered how Lo-Ruhamah must have felt when teams were being chosen for a game: "Ok, it's my turn. I think I'll show pity on Not Pitied and select her for my side!" Other examples could obviously be cited, but I'll restrain myself.

The Cost of God's Love

Unfortunately, marriage and motherhood did nothing to temper Gomer's promiscuous passions. She cheated on Hosea. She turned her back on him, spurned his love, and committed adultery. Who can imagine the pain Hosea endured as he stood by and watched his wife betray her vows and seek out sexual relations with other men?

Love, so we are told, like most everything else, surely has its limits. So who would dare speak ill of Hosea for divorcing Gomer? But he didn't. God's steadfast love, symbolically expressed in the action of Hosea shatters the mold. Indeed, it stretches the limits of credulity. How can I even begin to describe a love so deep that it would pursue a chronic fornicator even as she sought illicit pleasures in the arms of her paramour? Yet that is precisely what God told Hosea to do!

> And the LORD said to me, "Go again, love a woman who is loved by another man and is an adulteress, even as the LORD loves the children of Israel, though they turn to other gods and love cakes of raisins." So I bought her for fifteen shekels of silver and a homer and a lethech of barley. And I said to her, "You must dwell as mine for many days. You shall not play the whore, or belong to another man; so will I also be to you." (Hos. 3:1–3)

Hosea, playing the part of God, was to buy back his wayward and wanton wife. Gomer, playing the part of unfaithful Israel, was redeemed by the relentless love of her husband. It's easy to envision how the public auction would have proceeded:

"What am I to bid for the woman Gomer? She is beautiful and seductive and will bring pleasure to any man."

"Five shekels of silver," shouts one man from the crowd.

"Ten shekels of silver and a homer of barley," cries Hosea.

"Twelve shekels of silver and a homer and half a lethech of barley," another bids.

"Fifteen shekels of silver and a homer and lethech of barley," declares a persistent prophet.

"Do I hear another bid? The bid for Gomer is fifteen shekels of silver and a homer and lethech of barley. Going once. Going twice. Going three times. Sold to Hosea the prophet for fifteen shekels of silver and a homer and lethech of barley."

But it wasn't enough that God loved his people enough to redeem them from whoredom and idolatry and rebellion and infidelity. That would have clearly demonstrated the depths of his affection. But he went further and transformed his curses into blessings. This is seen in the changing of the children's names. Such is the power of God's love that Jezreel no longer means "God scatters" but "God plants" (Hos. 2:22). Lo-Ruhamah becomes Ruhamah, no longer "Not Pitied" but "Pitied." And Lo-Ammi, who lived under the reproach of being called "Not My People" is renamed Ammi, "My People."

Make no mistake. The redemptive love of Hosea for Gomer, that is, of God for Israel, was a foreshadowing of God's love for the church, for *you* and *me*. Let me be blunt: You and I were spiritual fornicators. We were worthy of eternal divorce in the depths of hell. But "in this the love of God was made manifest among us, that God sent his only Son into the world, so that we might live through him. In this is love, not that we have loved God but that he loved us and sent his Son to be the propitiation for our sins" (1 John 4:9–10).

Gomer was redeemed by Hosea for fifteen shekels of silver, a homer, and a lethech of barley. It was a beautiful illustration of the love God had for his people. But no amount of silver or gold, barley or corn, or any other earthly product could have been paid to deliver us from the slave market of sin and death. Perhaps with the story of Hosea and Gomer in mind, the apostle Peter reminds us that we "were ransomed from the futile ways inherited from your forefathers, not with perishable things such as silver or gold, but with the precious blood of Christ, like that of a lamb without blemish or spot" (1 Pet. 1:18–19)! Indeed, "God shows his love for us in that while we were still sinners, Christ died for us" (Rom. 5:8; see John 3:16; Gal. 2:20; Eph. 5:2).

Sending Jesus into the world was one thing. But sending him to *die* as the redemptive price for the souls of scurrilous spiritual adulterers like you and me is quite another—it is love beyond degree. Such is the steadfast love of God!

Forgiving a Repentant Prostitute

This love is also seen in the story of a wayward woman in Luke 7:36–50, which records Jesus's visit to the home of a Pharisee named Simon. A well-known prostitute crashes the dinner party, weeps profusely, anoints Jesus's feet, and wipes them dry with her hair. Simon is offended and declares, "If this man were a prophet, he would have known who and what sort of woman this is who is touching him, for she is a sinner" (Luke 7:39). Jesus then speaks to Simon, saying,

> "A certain moneylender had two debtors. One owed five hundred denarii, and the other fifty. When they could not pay, he cancelled the debt of both. Now which of them will love him more?"

Simon answered, "The one, I suppose, for whom he cancelled the larger debt." And he said to him, "You have judged rightly." Then turning toward the woman he said to Simon, "Do you see this woman? I entered your house; you gave me no water for my feet, but she has wet my feet with her tears and wiped them with her hair. You gave me no kiss, but from the time I came in she has not ceased to kiss my feet. You did not anoint my head with oil, but she has anointed my feet with ointment. Therefore I tell you, her sins, which are many, are forgiven—for she loved much. But he who is forgiven little, loves little." And he said to her, "Your sins are forgiven." Then those who were at table with him began to say among themselves, "Who is this, who even forgives sins?" And he said to the woman, "Your faith has saved you; go in peace." (7:41–50)

This is a remarkable story. Yet, the most remarkable thing about it isn't even in the Bible—it happened sometime *before* these events. Without a previous encounter between Jesus and the prostitute, which Scripture doesn't record for us, what Scripture does record is largely unintelligible. I realize that sounds strange, but bear with me. The encounter of Jesus with the unnamed woman in Luke 7 cannot have been the first time they met. What *she* did is meaningful only because of something *he* did. At some earlier time, perhaps on some isolated road or on a hillside, this lowly, shame-filled prostitute met Jesus, the friend of sinners.

I don't know what happened. Perhaps she heard him preach a sermon. Or maybe it was only one word he uttered. He might have prayed for her. Perhaps he touched her, the way he did the leper in Matthew 8. It's possible he only looked at her—a passing glance, a smile, an understanding nod of the head. In any case, it awakened in her the realization that this man was different; she sensed in him a quality and depth she'd never seen before.

Then again, it may be what he didn't do that affected her so profoundly: perhaps he didn't condemn her, as so many others had, and she felt from him no disdain, no contempt. Whatever he said or did, didn't say or didn't do, it changed her forever!

But before we go any further, let me introduce you to this woman. I think I know something about her. I think I understand her, if only a little.

The Cost of Human Love

This woman was, according to Luke 7:37, a "sinner," but not just any sort of sinner. Let's back up a couple of verses to Luke 7:34 where Jesus is quoting what his critics said of him: "The Son of Man has come eating and drinking, and you say, 'Look at him! A glutton and a drunkard, a friend of tax collectors and sinners!'" What could this possibly mean? Aren't we all sinners? Yes, but "sinners" here specifically means tax collectors and prostitutes. The one steals your money and the other sells her body for it. One can hardly imagine two more reprehensible occupations in the ancient world (they're not thought of highly today either!).

What's it like to be a prostitute? I know that's a strange question. I've gotten to know fairly well two women who were prostitutes before they came to know Jesus. I've spent time talking to them and hearing them tell in often agonizing terms what it means to sell your body to strangers. Their stories are never pretty and they seem to share several experiences in common.

Many of them at some point in their lives suffered horrible abuse. They have no idea what it's like to feel respect from other people. They only feel used and exploited. Most often they are ostracized by their families. The only people they trust are others who share their profession. They're pretty successful at putting on a good face and projecting a sexy image, but it's usually a facade that bears little resemblance to what's going on inside them. No matter how many times they "make love" (a horrible abuse of the term) with a customer, they don't know what it means to feel loved. One spoke to me of self-contempt that bordered on rage. Her body might go for five-hundred dollars an hour, but she felt utterly devalued and screamed at her soul. The shame was beyond words.

If this accurately describes the woman in Luke 7, what accounts for her love of Jesus, her joy in his presence, her unashamed and extravagant affection for him? Why did she regard him as her friend?

Here is a woman who probably never knew what it was like to be enjoyed as a person until she met Jesus, the friend of sinners. She knew all too well what it was like to be exploited as a prostitute but rarely, if ever, enjoyed. She probably never felt safe in the presence of a man until she came into the presence of Jesus, the friend of sinners. She'd never been able to give her heart to anyone, only her body. The only time she felt wanted was for someone else's perverse gratification—that is, until she met Jesus, the friend of sinners. He was probably the first man who ever chose to take note of her without wanting something in return.

He may not have used these words, but I wonder if she, through his gaze, heard him say something like this: "I like you. I delight in your femininity. I value you as a woman. And I look for nothing in return beyond your joy in enjoying my joy in you."

Little wonder that she couldn't have cared less what Simon or anyone else in that room might have thought. If you think all this is only speculation, I suggest that's because you haven't considered the devastation of repeated sexual immorality. Think about what sexual immorality does to a person. Paul warned the men at ancient Corinth that having sex with a prostitute was far more than merely physical. "Do you not know," said Paul, "that he who is joined to a prostitute becomes one body with her?" (1 Cor. 6:16). Every time you commit fornication you sin against your own body (1 Cor. 6:18). If this is true for a man who has sex with a prostitute, how much more so for the prostitute who has sex with everyone!

Each time she slept with another customer, it was as if she parceled out another piece of herself, as if she sliced off another layer of her identity and sold it to someone who couldn't care less. Who can overcome this kind of breakdown of the soul? Who can repair the disintegration of the spirit? Jesus, the friend of sinners. Perhaps never before did the famous words of Psalm 23:3 seem so relevant: "He restores my soul"! To all appearances, far beyond what had happened to her body, she had done irreparable damage to her soul—until she met the friend of sinners.

So let's turn our attention to what happened at this dinner party. We don't know what Simon's motive was in asking Jesus to join him for dinner that night. Curiosity? A desire to set a trap for Jesus or brag that Jesus had been in his home to enhance his status in the community?

All the guests, including Jesus, were "reclining at table" (Luke 7:37), which is to say they had removed their sandals and had stretched out on a cushion with their legs extended away from the table, most likely leaning on one arm, leaving the other free to handle the food. The opening words of the story are "And behold" (7:37). Luke's point is that what follows is shocking and utterly unexpected. It was one thing for the Pharisee to invite Jesus into his home; it was another thing altogether for this particular woman to enter uninvited into the home of a religious leader in the community.

The presence of uninvited guests was itself not unusual in those days. They would often come in and sit against the walls of the home, listening to dinner conversation and engaging the main guest in dialogue. What Luke portrays as shocking is the presence of a notorious sinner, a woman well-known in the community for her immoral lifestyle, here in the home of a highly respected and upright religious leader. As far as the people present were concerned, this woman should have known better than to defile the home of a Pharisee by entering in. In the public eye, she was the moral and spiritual antithesis of Simon.

Originally, her intention was to anoint the head of Jesus with perfume (which was customary). But evidently her emotions got the better of her. It would only be natural for her to be standing behind Jesus, above his feet, if he was reclining on a cushion. Thus, when she began to cry, her tears fell on his feet. In her anxiety to make up for this mishap, she ignored all social custom and proprieties, let down her hair (which a woman in that day was never to do in public), and wiped Jesus's feet dry. She then began to kiss his feet, a sign of deep reverence and gratitude, and anointed his feet again, this time with a costly perfume.

The irony here is so thick you can cut it with a knife. Simon is convinced that if Jesus were a true prophet, he would know who this woman is. The truth that he is a real prophet is seen from the fact that he knows precisely what Simon is thinking! In effect, what Simon is saying is this: "Jesus, doesn't she make you feel dirty? Doesn't she make you feel uncomfortable? Aren't you embarrassed to have her near you?" Our Lord must have shaken his head, heartbroken by such words. One can almost hear Jesus say, "Simon, if anyone makes me feel uncomfortable, it's you and your arrogant, legalistic religious spirit!"

Jesus then proceeds to tell a story about a moneylender who had two debtors. The point of the story isn't so much the gracious and forgiving character of the moneylender but the gratitude, or lack of gratitude, on the part of those whose debts are released. The question of who had more or fewer sins in a strictly quantitative sense is irrelevant. Who is to say whether Simon or the woman had committed more sins? A person with a legalistic spirit is surely capable of committing just as many sins as a prostitute!

The issue, rather, is one's subjective estimate of need. How desperate is Simon for the forgiveness that only Christ can give? How desperate and needy is the woman? Who has a greater conviction of sin, regardless of how many sins may be involved?

Note Simon's answer: "Well, I suppose . . ." A grudging concession. He's very cautious. Most likely he realizes he's been caught in a trap and his own shortcomings are about to be exposed in the presence of everyone present.

If you regard yourself as righteous, you will feel very little need for what Jesus can do. Your love for him, therefore, will be comparatively small. If you know yourself to be utterly unrighteous, your sense of need and desperation for what Jesus can do will be huge. And thus your love for him will be comparatively greater.

Jesus therefore uses a quantitative illustration to make a qualitative point. A person with only one sin who knows of that sin, sees it in the light of God's holiness, and is burdened with a genuine sense of guilt will love Jesus far more than a person who has a thousand sins but denies it, thinking himself to be righteous.

In other words, if you think you are righteous and that you have committed comparatively fewer sins, being forgiven will evoke little response; it simply won't register in your soul. But if you know yourself to be utterly unrighteous, alienated from God, and deserving of his wrath, regardless of how many sins you may have committed, forgiveness will have an immeasurable impact on your heart.

Let me be very, very clear about what is being said in this passage. After all, nothing less than eternity is at stake! Jesus is not saying that on the basis of her love, this prostitute will be forgiven. Our love for Jesus is not the cause of forgiveness. Jesus does not look at us and say, "Well, it's obvious you love me a lot. Therefore, I will forgive you of all your sins." No! Forgiveness is not the reward for love. How do we know this? Three things make it clear.

First, we see from Luke 7:42 that God's gracious cancellation of our debt precedes and leads to our love for him. Love is the fruit or the consequence of having one's debt cancelled and forgiven. If this were not the case, Jesus would not have used the future tense ("which of them will love him more?") but rather the past tense ("which of them had loved him more?")

Second, if we love God in order to be forgiven by him, the argument in this passage should be reversed. Instead of Jesus saying, "he who is forgiven little, loves little" (v. 47), he would have said, "he who loves little will be forgiven little."

Finally, faith saves, not works (not even the work of love). Jesus said it clearly in the final verse: "Your faith has saved you" (v. 50).

Jesus's point, then, is this: the prostitute's many sins have been forgiven, and we know this from the fact that she loves Jesus a lot. He infers from her love the reality of her forgiveness.

Our Christian Love

There are several important principles we learn from this story. I begin with the fact that genuine Christian love does not always come from those who appear most religious. Simon was culturally advanced, highly educated, well thought of in the community, and served as a religious leader and teacher. Yet he knew nothing of saving love. Sadly, Simon looked a lot like many who sit in our church services today. Even sadder still, Simon looked a lot like many who *preach* to those who sit in our church services today!

This story also shatters the notion that says, "I'm too sinful to be saved!" What it shows is that some are too righteous to be saved, which is to say, too righteous in their own estimation of themselves. I'm not saying that a religious leader like Simon can't be saved. But his self-righteousness prevents him from sensing his need for it, which cuts him off from salvation.

Furthermore, our love for Christ and our gratitude for his steadfast love and forgiving grace ought to be so intense and passionate that we care little for the social and cultural barriers that often prevent us from expressing it. Think of the slander and malicious gossip that the woman of Luke 7 was going to be subjected to. But she couldn't have cared less! Genuine love will always be willing to risk rebuke and upturned noses if need be to express what is felt in the heart. There were undoubtedly some present that evening who still looked on this prostitute with disdain and snobbish self-righteousness, but Jesus went out of his way to encourage her publicly with reassuring words. He announced where all could hear, "Your sins are forgiven" (v. 48). The reaction of those present is recorded in the next verse, but Jesus takes no note of it and proceeds to declare that her faith has saved her and that she should "go in peace" (v. 50).

It is also worth asking if a person who has genuinely been forgiven, who has truly been saved by the grace of Christ and been the object of his steadfast love, can fail to love and serve him. The answer is that though our love will at times falter and seem to fail, it will never disappear altogether. The flame will never fully die out. The idea that someone can be truly forgiven and then continue unabated, unconvicted, and unrepentant in sin is contrary not only to this passage but to the entire New Testament. Jesus, I believe, is laboring to tell us all that we know a person has been forgiven by how much that person loves him.

This story prompts me to ask, Who loves more? Who serves more? Who worships more? Is it the person whose religion is characterized by the command "Do" or the one who has heard God say, "Done"? The way to encourage and empower people for holiness is to preach the free forgiveness of sins and the steadfast love that is found in Jesus Christ. Knowing that his love for you is infinitely intense and never-ending and that your sins are finally and forever forgiven doesn't release you to do whatever you want or to sin as much as you please. It empowers you to love the forgiver all the more and to honor, serve, and obey him. We must work from life, not for life.

What would have motivated this woman to not revert to her old ways? What would have prevented her from walking out of Simon's house and at some point in the future giving herself yet again to prostitution? How was this woman to resist the temptation to sell her body yet again? The strength to say no to the allure of attention from men and the money she could make was the simple but glorious truth of the steadfast love of Jesus Christ. Jesus loves me! Jesus likes me! Jesus delights in me! God sings over me! I can almost hear her say to herself, "No matter how much money I might earn from sexual immorality, sin would serve only to deprive me of the incomparable and unparalleled delight of enjoying God and being loved by him, which is the truest form of love and greatest riches of all."

9

Overwhelmed by the Floodwaters of God's Love

ONE OF THE PRIMARY TASKS of any pastor is to prepare his people for suffering. I know that sounds strange, perhaps even a bit morbid, but there is a reason for it. Suffering, more than anything else in life, poses the greatest threat to our belief in God's goodness and the reality of his steadfast love for his people. When stuff happens, painful, distressing, discouraging stuff, our instinctive reaction is to blame God either for causing it or for not intervening to make it go away. When that happens, we take offense at God. We become bitter and resentful, and our faith starts to dwindle and weaken. Steadfast love strikes us as so obviously inconsistent with the trials, tribulations, pain, and distress that we encounter in life. We begin to wonder if God can be trusted with our lives.

That is why Romans 5:1–11 is so important. If I only had my choice of one paragraph in the entire Bible to demonstrate and unpack for you the reality of God's steadfast love, it would probably be this one. These verses are also important because they confront us with what on the surface appears to be a series of paradoxes. In other words, they run counter to how we think things should be. On the surface, it just doesn't appear to make much sense. But beneath the surface, it is grounded in reality. Let's first look closely at verses 1–5 in this chapter and then verses 6–11 in the next:

> Therefore, since we have been justified by faith, we have peace with God through our Lord Jesus Christ. Through him we have also obtained access by faith into this grace in which we stand, and we rejoice in hope of the glory of God. Not only that, but we rejoice in our sufferings, knowing that suffering produces endurance, and endurance produces character, and character produces hope, and hope does not put us to shame, because God's love has been poured into our hearts through the Holy Spirit who has been given to us.

By this point, Paul has repeatedly asserted in Romans that we have been justified by faith in Christ and therefore have peace with God. But if we are at peace with God, why doesn't he put an end to all our suffering? Why do we continue to encounter so much affliction and hardship and disappointment in life? Paul says we are at peace with God but it seems as if we are still at war. It seems as if he does nothing to remove the barriers we face. In fact, it almost appears as if he deliberately orchestrates our trials and painful experiences.

Paul also says, on the one hand, that we are to rejoice in our suffering and, on the other, that God has poured out his love for us through the Holy Spirit. If he really loves us, as Paul says he does, why must we continue to suffer in this life?

Related to this is Paul's twofold reference to our joy. On the one hand, he mentions our rejoicing in hope of the glory of God (Rom. 5:2). By this he means we have a sure and solid expectation that when this life is over, we will in some sense enter into and experience God's glory. But if that is true, how can he then say, on the other hand, that we are supposed to rejoice in our suffering? Isn't the hope of God's glory the expectation that suffering will stop? So how are we supposed to rejoice in something that we hope will one day forever cease? It seems as if we should despise suffering, knowing that one day it will all come to an end.

The Counterintuitive Nature of Christian Experience

Clearly, Christianity is at its very core counterintuitive. It runs contrary to what we, as humans, would expect. If you talk to any non-Christian and ask them, "Does it make sense that we should rejoice in our suffering?" they will first laugh in your face and then say, "No! Of course not!" But it doesn't stop there. Ask them if it makes sense to say, on the one hand, that God loves his children and, on the other hand, that he orchestrates their lives in such a way that they frequently encounter tribulation and trials. Once again, they will loudly protest, "No! Of course not!" After all, if God really loves us with steadfast affection, he will do everything in his power to shield us from suffering. At least, that's what our intuition tells us. But as I said, much of the Christian faith is counterintuitive.

Here in the opening verses of Romans 5, Paul is unpacking for us a handful of the many blessings and benefits of having been justified by faith in Christ. Because Jesus endured in our place the wrath and judgment we deserved, we are at peace with God. In addition to this, we have been given free and unhindered access to the grace by which God saved us. We stand in this grace. We are enveloped and saturated and sustained by this grace. On top of it all, Paul says in verse 2, we have the indescribably wonderful hope that when Christ finally returns, we will enter into and experience his glory (see Col. 3:4).

So think about it again before we go any further. The challenge for us, and especially for those who reject Christianity, is how we can be justified in God's sight, at peace with God, destined to share in his glory, and the objects of his unimaginably great, wonderful, and steadfast love all while he orchestrates our lives so that we are faced with tribulation and suffering. If you've ever wondered what is meant by the word "counterintuitive," that's it.

Joyful Boasting in Suffering

"We rejoice in our sufferings" (v. 3). If it were anyone else besides Paul who had the courage to write such an outlandish statement, I might be inclined to dismiss it and move on without comment. But it is Paul who said it, and we hear similar statements from Jesus, James, and Peter (see Matt. 5:10–12; James 1:2–4; 1 Pet. 1:6–7).

Now you might be inclined to respond to this by saying, "It may be easy for Paul to write those words, but if you had suffered like I did you wouldn't be so glib about pain and tribulation." Well, the fact of the matter is that the reverse is true. It is we who have no idea what it is like to suffer like Paul did. If you doubt this, read 2 Corinthians 11:23–27. Here Paul proclaims,

> Are they servants of Christ? I am a better one—I am talking like a madman—with far greater labors, far more imprison-ments, with countless beatings, and often near death. Five times I received at the hands of the Jews the forty lashes less

one. Three times I was beaten with rods. Once I was stoned. Three times I was shipwrecked; a night and a day I was adrift at sea; on frequent journeys, in danger from rivers, danger from robbers, danger from my own people, danger from Gentiles, danger in the city, danger in the wilderness, danger at sea, danger from false brothers; in toil and hardship, through many a sleepless night, in hunger and thirst, often without food, in cold and exposure.

This gives us a good picture of what Jesus, Paul, James, and Peter have in mind when they speak of "suffering" (Rom. 5:3). The word actually means "tribulation" or "affliction," but it can encompass virtually anything we face that threatens to undermine our confidence in God's love, goodness, and sovereignty. It is the hardships we endure, opposition we face, and pain we suffer simply for being followers of Jesus, be it physical beatings, verbal assaults, financial loss, or being targeted by cancel culture.

OK. *Endure* suffering. That I can understand. But *rejoice* in it? I can understand joyfully boasting that one day we will experience God's glory (Rom. 5:2), but how can Paul use the same word when it comes to our response to pain and suffering? Is he genuinely serious about this, and if so, how? Sadly, when hardship comes our way, such as losing a friend, job, or lucrative contract because of our Christian beliefs, we tend to respond with resentment, bitterness, and anger. Or we doubt God, wondering if he is really loving and compassionate after all. But Jesus, Paul, James, and Peter tell us to rejoice when facing this sort of adversity. Why? How?

I think there are at least two answers here in the text. In the first place, we can rejoice in our suffering because no matter what pain we encounter, we encounter it from a posture of standing in grace

(Rom. 5:2). We must always remind ourselves that whatever tribulations come our way, they strike us as we stand in grace, covered by God's unmerited favor and sustained by the power of his Holy Spirit. But this grace does not work magically in our lives. Its power comes from truth. We see and know and believe the truth of what God says and in this way we find strength to hold on. Second, we can rejoice in our sufferings because suffering sets in motion a chain of events that changes us and ultimately concludes in even greater hope. Let's now turn our attention to the first link in this chain: endurance.

Suffering Produces Endurance

Suffering "produces endurance" (Rom. 5:3). Those who suffer, says Tom Schreiner, are "toughened up"[1] so that they are able to bear up under the afflictions of life that come their way. But don't overlook the word "knowing" in verse 3. Suffering accomplishes nothing good in us if we don't reflect on how God uses it to build endurance and perseverance in our hearts. We can only rejoice in our suffering when we know that God makes use of it to produce within us a never-say-die mentality. This sort of joy doesn't just fall from heaven like manna. It doesn't suddenly and surprisingly appear in our lives willy-nilly. It only arises within us to the degree that we know that the fruit of suffering is a strengthened will and an intensified resolve to never give up. This is the truth through which the grace in which we stand gives us strength to endure.

Paul says that one way you resist the temptation to quit, one way you persevere, hang on, or endure, is by "knowing that suffering produces endurance." Your faith and resolve to hold fast to Jesus

---

1   Thomas R. Schreiner, *Romans*, 2nd ed. (Grand Rapids, MI: Baker Academic, 2018), 263.

get stronger through suffering in the same way that fire tempers steel. The flames of affliction are designed by God to make your faith unbreakable. And when you know this, you can gain the strength to keep going.

Endurance Produces Character

Character is the second link in this chain of transformation. Why should we place such high value on endurance? Because "endurance produces character" (v. 4). This is what Peter means when he writes,

> In this you rejoice, though now for a little while, if necessary, you have been grieved by various trials, so that the tested genuineness of your faith—more precious than gold that perishes though it is tested by fire—may be found to result in praise and glory and honor at the revelation of Jesus Christ. (1 Pet. 1:6–7)

Just as gold is purified of dross and every alloy when it passes through the literal fire in a furnace, so also your faith and confidence in God's steadfast love and sovereignty is purified when you persevere through suffering. And it is that enduring faith that Paul has in mind when he speaks of "character" (v. 4). He means that our determination to stay true to the gospel and our strength to resist temptation grow and deepen as the fire of hardship and tribulation burns away the hypocrisy and superficiality in our relationship with Jesus.

At the end of the day, as you look back on what you've endured, you experience this surge of joy knowing that your faith is real. Your relationship with Jesus is genuine and authentic and can persevere through anything the devil and this world might throw at you.

Character Produces Hope

The next link in this chain of personal transformation is hope (Rom. 5:4). How so? When you are transformed by enduring faithfully in the midst of hardship, it demonstrates to your soul that God is real and that your faith in his promises is not misplaced.

I can't count the number of times people have said to me that they fear they aren't true believers. They live in fear that they are hypocrites, that their faith is ill-founded and that this thing called "hope" they've put their confident expectation in will never ultimately come to pass. But Paul says that one of the beautiful things about our endurance of trials and tribulations is that it builds in us an ever-increasing confidence that we *will* inherit all the promises God has made.

Our Hope Is Sure

OK. But can we really know that our hope will not let us down? Can we really know with absolute assurance that God will come through for us on the day of judgment? Can we really know that his love for us is sincere and eternal and steadfast? Yes! Because God's word promises that "hope does not put us to shame."

You don't ever have to live in fear that when you stand before God on judgment day you will be filled with shame, consumed with regret, wishing that you had not chosen to follow Jesus. People often live their lives consumed with the fear of exposure. They are terrified of being seen for who they really are. The prospect of shame is overwhelming. But that never has to be the experience of God with his people. You need never live in anxious worry or doubt about whether he will be true to his word.

The Spirit Pours Out God's Love

So let me put the question to each of us once again. How do we know that our hope in Christ won't fall apart? What assurance do we have that it won't turn out to be empty and vain? How can we know with any degree of confidence that the final judgment won't utterly destroy us? Paul says that we know and can be assured of our future because God has poured out his love for us into our hearts through the Holy Spirit.

In verse 5, Paul speaks of "the love of God." Some English translations are unclear whether it is God's love for us or our love for God that Paul has in mind. But the English Standard Version, which reads, "God's love," is certainly correct and for two reasons.

First, the love of God is designed to be proof of the security of our hope. How could *our* love of God do that? Our love for God is often "faint and fitful."[2] If my hope is built on how well I love God, there will be times when I will be quite hopeless. Second, verses 6–11 are an obvious expansion of the nature of this love in verse 5.[3] There it is clearly—God's love for us as demonstrated by the gracious gift of his Son to die in our stead.

So Paul tells us that God's love "has been poured into our hearts." The verb "poured out" is used elsewhere of the spilling of wine (Luke 5:37), the shedding of Christ's blood (Matt. 26:28), and the pouring out of the Holy Spirit at Pentecost (Acts 10:45). More graphic still is its use in Acts 1:18 of the fate of Judas: "Now this man acquired a field with the reward of his wickedness, and falling headlong he burst open in the middle and all his bowels *gushed out.*"

2   J. I. Packer, *Knowing God* (Downers Grove, IL: InterVarsity Press, 1993), 118

3   We see this from the opening word in verse 6, "for," an indication that what follows in verses 6–11 is the ground for our confidence in the truth of verses 1–5.

Thus, in Romans 5, Paul is emphasizing the unstinting, boundless lavishness with which God has flooded our hearts. "The hearts of believers," writes John Murray, "are regarded as being suffused with the love of God; it controls and captivates their hearts."[4] The steadfast love of God that is poured out in our hearts is like an ever-flowing, self-replenishing stream of life-giving water in a dry and deserted land.

This is an exuberant communication of God's love. The love of God, writes Charles Hodge, "does not descend upon us as dew drops, but as a stream which spreads itself abroad through the whole soul, filling it with the consciousness of his presence and favor."[5] God wants your heart to be inundated by wave after wave of his fatherly affection, so effusively poured out that you feel compelled to request that he pull back lest you drown in his passion! Paul is not talking "of faint and fitful impressions," says J. I. Packer, but of "deep and overwhelming ones."[6] The famous evangelist Dwight L. Moody (1837–1899) knew precisely what this meant. He had an experience of God's love that was so profound that he had to ask God to "stay his hand," lest he die.[7]

It's also important to note that Paul uses the perfect tense of the verb. Packer explains that this implies

a settled state consequent upon a completed action. The thought is that knowledge of the love of God, having flooded our hearts, *fills them now,* just as a valley once flooded remains full of water. Paul assumes that all his readers, like himself, will be

4   John Murray, *The Epistle to the Romans* (Grand Rapids, MI: Eerdmans, 1971), 165.
5   Charles Hodge, *Commentary on the Epistle to the Romans* (Grand Rapids, MI: Eerdmans, 1974), 135.
6   Packer, *Knowing God*, 118.
7   William R. Moody, *The Life of D. L. Moody* (New York: F. H. Revell, 1900), 149.

living in the enjoyment of a strong and abiding sense of God's love for them.[8]

In other words, God's love doesn't leak. Unlike the waters of Noah, which receded after a time, God's steadfast love perpetually remains at flood stage in our souls. The Holy Spirit works to evoke and stimulate in your heart the overwhelming conviction that God loves you. And the amplitude and immensity of God's devotion is not abstract and generic but concrete and personal, not for everyone in general but for *you* in particular.

It is difficult to describe more precisely what Paul is saying here. Perhaps this is because he's not talking about knowledge that we gain by inference from a body of evidence. Neither deduction nor induction can account for what he has in mind. Empirical observation doesn't yield the assurance of being God's beloved. We aren't dealing here with a logical truth that can be concluded from certain premises.

Let me explain. We read in John 3:16 that "God so loved the world, that he gave his only Son, that whoever believes in him should not perish but have eternal life." Thus, I can logically arrive at the conclusion that God loves me. Here's how:

Major premise: God loves the world.
Minor premise: I'm part of the world.
Conclusion: Therefore, God loves me.

And of course, that's true. Again, how can I know I have eternal life? I can know it by simple logic:

---

8   Packer, *Knowing God*, 118.

Major premise: God says that whoever believes in Jesus has eternal life.

Minor premise: I believe in Jesus.

Conclusion: Therefore, I have eternal life.

These are conclusions we draw from thinking. They are the product of unbreakable logic. And that is wonderful. But that isn't what Paul is saying here in Romans 5:5. He isn't talking about logic (although he soon will in verses 6–11). He's talking about experience. He doesn't appeal to an argument but to a sensation produced in our hearts by the Holy Spirit. I know this makes some people uncomfortable. They don't like feelings. They don't trust emotion. But there is no escaping what Paul says.

Notice that Paul does not say that God has enlightened our minds to know that he loves us (although I'm so incredibly grateful he does that too). Nor does he say that he has taught us by irrefutable reasoning that God loves us. He says, instead, that God has poured out into our hearts, through the Holy Spirit, the reality of his love for us. Not in our minds but in our hearts. Not instructed or explained but poured out.

This is an altogether subjective, experiential reality. Earlier we spoke of certain Christian doctrines as being counterintuitive. Well, this is profoundly intuitive. It is an awakening in our deepest emotions and feelings of the reality of God's abiding and joyful affection for his children. You won't always be able to explain it in words, but you know undeniably and inescapably in your heart that God really does love you.

That doesn't mean this love has no objective foundation. It most certainly does. The objective proof or grounds for this love is precisely what Paul will proceed to say in verses 6–8. There he points us to the sacrificial, substitutionary death of Jesus in our place. So don't ever think that your hope is only as good as your ability to experience or feel God's love for you. He most assuredly wants you to feel it, but even when you don't, you can know his love is real and sure and certain by reminding yourself of the lengths to which he went in making you his child: the death of his own Son on your behalf.

We will look at the carefully reasoned explanation of the objective grounds for our hope, namely, the death of Jesus, in subsequent chapters. But here in Romans 5:5 Paul is talking about an internal, subjective, experiential, undeniable surge of confidence that God not only loves us but likes us!

God's remedy for your doubt and fear and anxiety is the work of the Holy Spirit in creating in your heart an irrefutable and inescapable sense of his love for you. This does not happen because of anything that any human being can do. I can't do it by writing a book. You can't do it by reading it. Only the Holy Spirit can do it. That is why Paul prays as he does in 2 Thessalonians 3:5, "May the Lord direct your hearts to the love of God and to the steadfastness of Christ.

This short verse is important because it reminds us of two things: first, that there are inescapable obstacles to our capacity to feel God's affection for us, and second, that if we are to experience that love, it is God himself who must "direct" our "hearts" into the enjoyment of it.

He can and will do it in all of our hearts, even those of the most abused and neglected of souls. Some of you have been so traumatized in your youth, or perhaps today in your adulthood, that you find yourself seemingly incapable of believing that the God of Scripture cares anything about you. But the Holy Spirit can heal whatever suffering you've endured and bring to your heart the unshakable conviction that you are a beloved child of God. This experience does not come from being raised by Christian parents. It does not come because you have a seminary education. It comes directly and immediately by something the Spirit does in your heart.

And we must never diminish or deny this experience simply because it is an experience. Remember: it is an experience that flows from a concrete, empirically verifiable, objective event that occurred in time-and-space history when Jesus gave his life for you on the cross. So you don't have to empty your mind or work yourself into an altered state of consciousness to experience this truth. Just look to the cross of Christ, where God's steadfast love poured out for you is on clear display.

10

The "Much More" Love of God

HAVE YOU EVER READ a passage of Scripture and immediately recognized yourself in the text? I have. It happens every time I read Romans 5:6–11:

> For while we were still weak, at the right time Christ died for the ungodly. For one will scarcely die for a righteous person—though perhaps for a good person one would dare even to die—but God shows his love for us in that while we were still sinners, Christ died for us. Since, therefore, we have now been justified by his blood, much more shall we be saved by him from the wrath of God. For if while we were enemies we were reconciled to God by the death of his Son, much more, now that we are reconciled, shall we be saved by his life. More than that, we also rejoice in God through our Lord Jesus Christ, through whom we have now received reconciliation.

You may wonder how I could see myself in this passage, given the fact that the name "Sam Storms" does not appear in it. Oh, but

I'm there. I'm in it, writ large. I am the one who is "weak." I am the one who is "ungodly." I am the "sinner." I am God's "enemy."[1]

But perhaps my use of the present tense "I am" is misleading. It's more accurate to say, I *was* weak, ungodly, sinful, and an enemy of God. Because of the steadfast love of God and what Jesus did for me on the cross, I am now strong in his strength. I am now godly insofar as I have been declared righteous because of the righteousness of Jesus. Although I am still a sinner, that is not my fundamental identity. I now, through the power of the Holy Spirit, don't have to sin. And I am no longer God's enemy but his friend, his child forever and ever.

If you cannot see yourself in these descriptive terms, you will never understand Christianity. You will never know God. You will never feel the thrill of being made a recipient of God's amazing, reconciling, forgiving grace and steadfast love.

When God looked at me, he saw someone who was profoundly weak, ungodly, and sinful—an enemy. But his love for me was so great and beyond imagination that he sent his Son, Jesus Christ, to die for weak, ungodly, sinful enemies like me. Because of this, God was free to justify me, to declare me righteous through faith in the death of Christ Jesus. I am now reconciled to him, one with him, found in him, never to endure another second of alienation and hatred.

That is the fundamental message of these Spirit-inspired, Christ-exalting words in verses 6–11. In this chapter, we have the privilege of digging deeply into these verses, laying our hands on our hearts, and declaring, "Although I was once weak, ungodly,

---

1 Some of what follows has been adapted from my book *Kept for Jesus: What the New Testament Really Teaches about Assurance of Salvation and Eternal Security* (Wheaton, IL: Crossway, 2015). Used by permission.

sinful, and an enemy of God, I have been reconciled to him by the blood of his Son!"

If You Wake Up Tomorrow, Will You Still Be a Christian?

I hope nothing ominous happens to you today, but it may. You may die in your sleep. I pray that will not happen. But it may. You may wake up tomorrow and discover that you have cancer. You may wake up tomorrow and be told by your child that she experiences same-sex attraction, and she doesn't know what to do about it, and neither do you. You may wake up tomorrow and be told by your spouse that he has decided to leave you and start a new life with someone else.

Those would be horrible ways to start a day. But my question for you now is simply this: When you wake up tomorrow morning, no matter what else may have happened during the night, and no matter what else anyone else may have decided to do, will you still be a Christian? Will you still be considered righteous in the sight of God? Will you still be his child, destined for an eternity with him in the new heaven and new earth? Paul has declared that we have peace with God and therefore have hope that on the final day we will experience God's glory (Rom. 5:1–2). But how can I be sure that I'll make it that far? How can I know that I'll persevere from now until then? How can I know that the faith I now have I'll have on that final day?

Many of you right now are saying to yourselves, "Sam, what a dumb question to ask! Of course I'll wake up a Christian. If I went to sleep as one, I'll wake up as one. I'm confident and secure in my relationship with God and I know that his love for me is steadfast and certain. I will most assuredly persevere in my relationship with Jesus until the end."

Others of you might be saying to yourself, "I certainly hope so. But I can't be sure. Who knows if my sin may have pushed God beyond his breaking point and he has decided during the night or on the previous day to cut ties with me and to sever my relationship with Jesus? Who knows if I may wake up and discover that I've lost faith in Jesus and no longer consider him Lord of my life?"

I'm telling you right now that if you and I wake up tomorrow and discover that we are still saved, justified, born-again believers in Jesus—and we will—it is only because God, on the basis of his steadfast love, made a commitment to us that he would finish the job that he began when we first trusted in Jesus. "And I am sure of this," said Paul in his letter to the Philippians, "that he who began a good work in you will bring it to completion at the day of Jesus Christ" (Phil. 1:6).

I could stop right there and declare that this theological debate is over. God's elect, born-again children will never wake up and discover that they are no longer Christians. This issue, of course, has been debated and discussed for centuries. Entire denominations have been built by identifying with one or the other view. Southern Baptists, Presbyterians, and people in most independent Bible churches affirm that our salvation is secure in God's love. The Assemblies of God, Methodists, Nazarenes, and the Churches of Christ, among others, believe that it is possible for a Christian to lose or forfeit one's salvation. The former believe that once you are truly saved, you are always saved. The latter do not.

I identify with those who believe that a true born-again, justified-by-faith-in-Jesus believer is eternally secure in the salvation that God has granted by his grace. This is an issue that arises several times in Romans, as it does here in Romans 5:6–11. We will now look at this passage to learn two things: (1) the character of God's steadfast love for us (5:6–8) and (2) the consequences of God's love for us (5:9–11).

The Character of God's Steadfast Love for Us

First, it's important that you see the connection between verses 6–11 and what has preceded in verse 5. Paul states in verse 5 that our hope in God will never, ever prove futile. It will never let us down or disappoint us. We know this because God loves us and has poured this love into our hearts through the Holy Spirit. Our hope is as secure as God's love is immutable and steadfast.

But there is more. Paul appears to be saying that since God has demonstrated his love for us by sending Jesus to die for our sins, it follows that he will do everything necessary to make certain that we are safely and securely preserved all the way to the end. But how do we know God loves us in this way? What is the historical, empirical, objective foundation of our confidence in that love? Paul's answer comes in verses 6–11. Here, Paul proceeds to answer two questions. First, when did Christ die? Second, and more important still, for what kind of people did Christ die?

I'll be brief in my answer to the first question. Paul says in verse 6 that it was "at the right time" that Christ died for us. Simply put, the death of Jesus was no accident, no quirk of fate, no blip on the pages of history that caught everyone by surprise. In Galatians 4:4, Paul says it was "when the fullness of time had come" that God sent forth his Son to die. Both of these phrases mean it was in God's time or it was when the Father determined for him to die. The death of Jesus didn't sneak up on God and catch him by surprise, perhaps when the Father was looking the other way, dealing with more important issues on the other side of globe. But even so, knowing when Christ died is of secondary importance to understanding the nature of those he gave his life for.

This second question is one that I've already answered briefly. In this passage, Paul gives us a fourfold description of the kind of people Jesus died for. First, they were "weak" people (v. 6). The NIV translates this as "powerless" while the King James Version renders it, "without strength." By using this term, Paul is referring to spiritually and morally impotent people who are unable to prepare themselves for acceptance with God, unable to prove themselves worthy of Christ's sacrifice, helpless to do or say anything that might attract God's love. You may remember the famous saying that "God helps those who help themselves." When it comes to salvation, Paul disagrees: God helps those who are utterly and absolutely helpless!

Second, the people Jesus died for are "ungodly" people (v. 6). We see this same thing back in Romans 4:5 where Paul says that God "justifies the ungodly." Jesus didn't die for Bible readers or truth tellers or tithers or people who regularly pray. He didn't die for nor does he justify Baptists, Presbyterians, charismatics, Methodists, Jews, or Gentiles. The only people Jesus died for and the only people God justifies are "ungodly" people! He didn't die for only Republicans or only Democrats or only those who do not identify with either political party. He didn't die only for those who have at least $500,000 in their 401(k) or a graduate degree from an accredited university. The only people he died for were "ungodly" people.

To be ungodly surely means we are unlike God. God is infinitely pure and holy and righteous, and we are not. But to be ungodly means more than that we differ from God. It also means we stand opposed to God. As Paul will say in verse 10, we are his "enemies." When you say that a person is un-American, you mean more than that they live outside of America. You mean they embrace an ideology that is antithetical to American principles. Similarly, to be ungodly means we dislike God. Indeed, we hate God. When he says yes, we say no. When he says no, we say yes. These are the kind of people Jesus died for!

Third, Jesus died for "sinners" (v. 8). There are not two classes of people in the world: those who sin and those who don't. All are ungodly, spiritually impotent, defiant sinners. And it is these kinds of people Jesus died for and God justifies by faith.

Fourth, Jesus died for his "enemies" (v. 10). Don't water down that term. It means everything you think it means: rebellious, insolent, haughty, arrogant, self-righteous, repulsive, disobedient, and defiant to God and all that he represents and says. And it is not simply that we are enemies of God but also that before we are forgiven and justified, God is an enemy to us. We are not simply opposed to God. He is opposed to us.

If you quickly slide past this fourfold description of the human race you will just as readily slide past the glorious nature of God's steadfast love. God's love will never be seen for the stupendous, incomprehensibly glorious thing that it is until you come to grips with your own fallen nature apart from his grace. Sadly, people today think of themselves not as weak but as strong and competent, not as ungodly but godlike, not as sinners but as righteous, not as enemies but friends. Let's now go even deeper into Paul's argument as it unfolds in verses 7–8.

Who is this so-called "righteous" person one will scarcely die for? Keep in mind that by "righteous" and "good," Paul is speaking in purely human terms. He has already told us in Romans 3 that no one is righteous or good in God's sight. He is describing people as we see them, not as God sees them. The "righteous" person is the civil, law-abiding person who fulfills his duty. This person meets their obligations and fulfills their promises. This is the kind of person who evokes your respect but not necessarily your affection. This person is lawful but not gentle, firm but not friendly. It is unlikely that you would give your life for that individual. Your admiration does not go so far that you would be willing to sacrifice your life for him.

The "good" person you would "perhaps" die for is the righteous person who is also kind, loving, and altruistic. This person evokes your admiration and your affection, both your respect and your love. For such a person, perhaps, you might be willing to die. You are slightly more inclined to sacrifice your life for that kind of individual than you would for those who, in the eyes of people, are merely righteous.

"But God"! There it is, those glorious words of contrast. God shows (or demonstrates) and puts on public display his steadfast love for us by sending his beloved Son to die, not for righteous people, not for good people, not for intelligent, hard-working, church-attending people, but for sinful enemies. What you and I would only reluctantly do for a good person, God joyfully, spontaneously, abundantly, and freely does for evil people. The love of God thus runs counter to every known or implied rule of human behavior.

Mothers, would you gladly die for the sake of your child? Yes! But would you die for the person who kidnapped and murdered your child? No. Fathers, would you willingly give your life for the sake of your child? Yes! But would you die for the sake of the one who brutally abused your child? No.

But that is what God did! He didn't send his Son to die for those who loved him or sought him or served him. He sent his Son to die for the very people who murdered him, for those who spat in his face and despised him. That is the character of God's steadfast love for us.

Imagine a Christian in conversation with a nonbeliever. When the nonbeliever hears this, he says, "That's no big deal. I have a son who is in North Korea serving the poor. He has been thrown into a prison and given a life sentence. I would gladly give my life for him so that he might return home." The Christian responds, "Yes, but would you do the same for the North Koreans who arrested and tortured and imprisoned him?" That is what God did for us.

What was it about us that attracted our Lord Jesus Christ? What was it about us that moved the heart of our heavenly Father to send his Son to die? Was it in response to our plea for help? Our good looks? Our potential for virtuous, self-sacrificial deeds? To salvage what little divine spark still flickered in our souls? No. Nothing in us, about us, or done by us could serve to move God's heart. The only explanation of why God sent his Son to die for us is that he wanted to. He loved us because he loved us.

Let's linger for a moment on the word in verse 8 translated by the ESV as "shows," perhaps better rendered "demonstrates." The cross of Christ is the demonstration of God's love, not its procuring cause. Christ's death on the cross isn't what moved God's heart to love you. It was God's heart of love for you that led and stirred him to send his Son to die. Jesus doesn't stand before the Father pleading, "Oh, Father, I died for them; will you not therefore now love them?" No! He declares that God loved them, therefore he—God's Son—died for them.

The Consequences of God's Steadfast Love for Us

When we looked at Romans 5:5 in chapter 9 of this book, I pointed out that Paul was not speaking in strictly logical terms, as if he wanted to prove a point. He described there an experience. It wasn't an argument he was attempting to prove but a feeling of the reality of God's love that the Holy Spirit awakens in us. But now, in verses 9–10, Paul does make a logical argument, and it is irrefutable and airtight.

He begins in verse 9 with a proposition. He makes his case on the basis of God's greatest expression of love for us. God justified us because of Jesus's work on the cross.

Of course, Paul has said clearly on multiple occasions before that it is only if we believe and have faith in Jesus's work that God declares us to be righteous in his sight. On the basis of this truth, Paul can assure us that when the day of final judgment comes, we will still be "saved from the wrath of God" (v. 9). God the Father himself has worked in the past decisively through the death of Christ and will therefore work in the future infallibly through the life of Christ to rescue us from his wrath (v. 10). In fact, it is "much more" certain that we will be saved and delivered from God's wrath on that day.

How can Paul say that? What is the basis or ground for this assertion? There are at least two sorts of logical reasoning in Scripture: reasoning from the lesser to the greater and reasoning from the greater to the lesser. One example of the former is in the Sermon on the Mount, where Jesus says, "Or which one of you, if his son asks him for bread, will give him a stone? Or if he asks for a fish, will give him a serpent? If you then, who are evil, know how to give good gifts to your children, how much more will your Father who is in heaven give good things to those who ask him!" (Matt. 7:9–11).

An example of reasoning from the greater to the lesser is found in Romans 8:32, which reads, "He who did not spare his own Son but gave him up for us all, how will he not also with him graciously give us all things?" If the greatest, most costly, and most sacrificial thing God could do for us was to send his Son to suffer and die on a cross, does it not stand to reason that he would then do those things to keep us saved, which, by comparison, are far easier, far less sacrificial, and far less demanding? Yes!

But there is more to the argument than that. He doesn't just do this for good, loving, and holy people. He does it for weak, ungodly, and sinful enemies. If the greater task was for God to send his Son to die for us while we were his hate-filled enemies, how much easier and more readily would he save us from the coming wrath now that we are his friends, indeed, his sons and daughters? If Christ died for his enemies, he will surely save his friends.

Further, if Christ loved us as much as he did while we were helpless, weak, ungodly, sinful, enemies, how much more will he love us now that by his grace we are justified, righteous in him, adopted as children, and reconciled to his heart! Will the God who loved us and saved us when we hated him turn his back and desert us now that we love him? No. He saved us while we hated him and so it is certain that he will keep us secure now that we love and trust him.

Getting the consent of his holy and righteous nature to send his Son to die for you while you were ungodly was the greatest and most costly, demanding thing God could ever do. By comparison, keeping you saved is a breeze! How could we possibly think that God was willing to do the greatest thing for us but is now unwilling to do something far less?

If there ever were a time for God not to love you and me, a time to forsake and desert us and cast us aside, it would have been when we were aliens, opposed to him, at war with him, unreconciled to him. But now you and I are no longer unreconciled; we are his children. No longer are you at enmity with God but in love with him. It is logically, theologically, and biblically impossible that God would love you less now, now that you are his child, than he did when you were his enemy.

So what does Paul mean when he says we will be saved "by his life," that is, the life of Jesus? He's already said in verse 10 that we were reconciled to God by the death of Jesus. Now he says that it is even "much more" certain and sure that we "shall be saved by his life." This is most likely a reference both to the resurrection of Jesus as well as his heavenly intercession on our behalf. Hebrews 7:25 shows us just that: "Consequently, he is able to save to the uttermost those who draw near to God through him, since he always lives to make intercession for them."

Correcting a Misunderstanding

I've often heard people describe our value in God's sight by referring to us as treasures and pearls, as if our preciousness is what moved his heart to send Jesus to die for us. But if that is the case, what is the purpose of grace? The cross is an expression of grace because those Christ died for merited only wrath and hell. If those he died for were "treasures" God valued, why would God need to show grace to them? Would we not, then, merit his atoning sacrifice? If God saw something in us that stirred him to send Jesus for us, the gift of his Son ceases to be grace and becomes a matter of paying what is owed.

When we ask, "Who were we that led God to do this for us?" the only answer is, "You were hell-deserving rebels who had no claim on anything in God other than to be the recipients and objects of eternal wrath. God did this for you not because you were a treasure or because of anything in you; indeed, it was in spite of what was in you. God did this for you solely because of what was in *him*, namely, sovereign, free, gracious, steadfast love for those who deserved only to be hated."

When people think about why God smiled on them in the cross of Christ they should say, "It certainly wasn't because of anything in me. In fact, I should have brought only a frown of judgment to his face. That he should have smiled in redemptive love is traceable only to his sovereign and gracious good pleasure. Thanks be to God that he has chosen to make a treasure out of a moral dung heap. It was not because I was a treasure but in spite of my being a moral dung heap that he was moved to love me in the first place."

It is one thing to say that we have value as image bearers (and we do); it is altogether another thing to suggest that what moved God to love us and send his Son to die in our stead was our value as image bearers. What stirred the heart of God to send his Son was the free and sovereign choice of love. I don't believe God said, "Well, [or perhaps even "Wow"], these fallen humans are of such worth that I now feel love for them and, because of this worth, I will send Jesus to die for them and redeem them."

I think God would instead have said something like, "Well, these fallen humans deserve only my wrath and eternal damnation. They have squandered all that I gave them. They are helpless to do anything that might merit my favor. They are ungodly, in the sense that they are both morally unlike me and relationally against me. They are sinful in thought, word, and deed. They are my enemies. But I am determined to glorify myself through them. Therefore, in spite of the fact that they don't deserve anything other than hell, in spite of the fact that if I were to immediately consign every one of them to eternal condemnation I would be perfectly just and fair and righteous in doing so, I am going to love them. I am going to choose to have compassion on them. I am going to take these immoral wretches and make them treasures and trophies of my grace." That is, in my opinion, what Scripture is saying to us, particularly in Romans 5:6–11.

Nothing less than the precious blood of Christ was required because of the immeasurable heights and holy demands of God's character. It was the value of God's holiness that could be satisfied with nothing less than the life, death, and resurrection of his sinless Son. No other sacrifice would suffice, not because those redeemed are so valuable that an immeasurably high price was required but because their sin was so evil and the one they sinned against was so gloriously good that only the blood of Jesus could appease and make amends and fully satisfy the justice of such a God.

Worship!

The same word used in Romans 5:2 to describe our joyful boasting and exultation in the hope of God's glory is the word used in verse 3 to describe our joyful boasting and exultation in our tribulation. And it is one more time the very same word now used in verse 11 to describe our joy and exultation in God for all he has done for us in Jesus. But note carefully how and on what basis this is done: it is "through our Lord Jesus Christ." There is no such thing as acceptable, God-honoring worship that is not grounded in, focused on, and accomplished by the person and work of Jesus Christ. So, I say, let's rejoice! Let's boast in God and his steadfast love. Let us now exult in him so that he may be exalted in us.

11

The Incalculable, Insurmountable, Sin-Killing, Soul-Preserving Love of God

I HAVE A GUARANTEED ANSWER to one of the most pressing questions you will ever ask. I have a remedy for what may well be the greatest fear in your heart.[1] The question and the fear are the same: Will God's love for me one day dissipate and disappear? Is there a limit to his love? Is it even remotely possible that one day he will simply grow tired of me and give up? Could the adjective "steadfast" be an illusion? According to Scripture, the answer is a resounding "No"!

The fear that cripples, paralyzes, and haunts many hearts is that no matter how good it may be now to enjoy God's love for us, this love won't last. No matter how heartwarming it may be to think of God's affection and delight for me, hell-deserving sinner that

---

1   Some of what follows has been adapted from my book *Kept for Jesus: What the New Testament Really Teaches about Assurance of Salvation and Eternal Security* (Wheaton, IL: Crossway, 2015), 59–70, 80–85. Used by permission.

I am, there's likely coming a day when it will all end. No matter how often I remind myself that God is good and always keeps his promises, I'm stuck with the inescapable reality of my own sinful soul and the countless times I treat God's grace and love with contempt. Surely, or so I say to myself, God will one day get fed up with me and pull the plug on my salvation. And honestly, I couldn't blame him if he did.

When I ask people why they struggle with this fear, among the many answers given, three often stand out above the rest. First, it's common for people to say, "My enemies are too many and too powerful. The deck is stacked against me. There are powerful people and even spiritual forces that threaten to expose me for the fraud that I am. They may step in between me and God and threaten to tell him how pathetic I am when it comes to loving him and obeying him. It may be people who pass themselves off as my friends. It may be a family member. It may be someone who really hates me. And Satan is surely there all the time seeking to undo what God's grace has done."

If this fear wasn't bad enough, there's yet another. This fear says, "My needs are just too many; they are, quite simply, overwhelming. To stay the course, persevere in faith, and find the strength not to quit requires so much that I seriously doubt if God is either able or willing to keep on supplying me with what I need. Surely, at some point, the well is going to run dry. Surely, at some point, God is going to put a plug on the fountain of mercy and grace that has flowed so freely for so long."

Finally, the third fear laments, "Even if something can be done about my enemies, and even if I can be convinced that God can meet my needs, my sins are simply too numerous. I keep doing the same stupid, selfish things over and over again. When I think of how ungrateful I am, how prone I am to repeat past failures, how prideful and lustful and weak and addicted I am, I find it almost impossible to believe that a God worth his salt would bother to put up with me any longer and continue to invest his energy in my life."

So how long will God's love last? A lot of Christians, when asked that question, shrug their shoulders in ignorance or cringe in fear that it won't last much longer. These concerns, these anxieties, these reasons why we doubt the durability of God's love aren't theological abstractions concocted by some pointy-headed apostle who got bored sitting in his first-century ivory tower. They are all too real, and we each face them in our own way almost daily.

But each one of these three fears that leads to doubt and anxiety and, in some people, despair, are raised by Paul in Romans 8:31–39 and then carefully and thoroughly refuted by him. So let's follow the apostle as he takes up, one by one, each of our fears and finally and forever puts them to rest by telling us what God has done and will do for us in Jesus Christ. Paul writes,

> What then shall we say to these things? If God is for us, who can be against us? He who did not spare his own Son but gave him up for us all, how will he not also with him graciously give us all things? Who shall bring any charge against God's elect? It is God who justifies. Who is to condemn? Christ Jesus is the one who died—more than that, who was raised—who is at the right hand of God, who indeed is interceding for us. Who shall separate us from the love of Christ? Shall tribulation, or distress, or persecution, or famine, or nakedness, or danger, or sword? As it is written, "For your sake we are being killed all the day long; we are regarded as sheep to be slaughtered." No, in all these things we are more than conquerors through him who loved us. For

I am sure that neither death nor life, nor angels nor rulers, nor things present nor things to come, nor powers, nor height nor depth, nor anything else in all creation, will be able to separate us from the love of God in Christ Jesus our Lord.

I have to tell you that when I read this passage, I get the feeling that Paul is actually issuing to each of us a stern challenge. It's almost as if he says: "Go ahead. Come on, Christian, take your best shot. Voice your concerns. Tell God why you can't trust his love. Throw at him your most powerful and persuasive objections. Lay it out why you fear that his love isn't steadfast and may soon fade into little more than a distant echo. Bring it on! I'm ready for you!" OK, Paul, here goes.

"My Enemies Are Too Numerous and Too Powerful"

First of all, my enemies are too numerous and powerful and so committed to undoing everything God has done, I don't think I stand much of a chance in the long run. Satan is too clever, my enemies are too abundant, and others hate me so deeply that I'm not sure I can hold up much longer. I'm surrounded by people who would love nothing more than to see me fail miserably.

Paul's response to this is simple and straight to the point. He asks each of us a question: "If God is for us, who can be against us?" (v. 31).

In asking this question, Paul is not suggesting that we have no adversaries. He had dozens, perhaps hundreds, of them. They beat, whipped, slandered, stoned, and imprisoned him and did everything they could to undermine his work and ministry. In this passage, Paul also lists the types of adversaries and opposition that we may all face, citing tribulation, distress, persecution, famine, nakedness, danger, and sword (v. 35). It's safe to say you will never reach a stage of the Christian life in which you no longer have enemies or face opposition. In fact, with spiritual increase and success, our enemies multiply!

Paul's point is simply that no adversary or enemy is of any account because God is for us. Since God is for us, to use the words of Romans 8:28, all things work together for our ultimate spiritual good, even those things our enemies intend for our harm! No enemy can ever achieve what they arrogantly claim when they attack us.

Notice also that Paul doesn't simply ask the question, "Who is against us?" His question is, "If God is for us, who can be against us?" In other words, if the God who, according to Romans 8:29–30, foreknew and predestined and called and justified and glorified us, if *that* God is for us, who can be against us?

So who precisely is that God? What kind of God are we talking about? Psalm 115:3 describes him as being "in the heavens" and doing "all that he pleases." And in Isaiah 46:9–10 he describes himself, saying, "I am God, and there is no other; I am God, and there is none like me, declaring the end from the beginning and from ancient times things not yet done, saying, 'My counsel shall stand, and I will accomplish all my purpose'" (see Dan. 4:34-35).

Let's recall why Paul asked his rhetorical question. He was confronting our fear of the collective power of the many forces and enemies amassed against us. Paul knew that there will always be a person or people out there whose ridicule and hostility and rejection you feel unable to face. Paul knows how inhibiting and paralyzing such fear can be. So he calls on us to think. Think about all your enemies and all their disdain for you; put it on one side of the scales of balance. Now put the God of Romans 8, Psalm 115, and Isaiah 46 on the other side. Who is weightier? Who is mightier?

Who is more powerful? "Greater is he who is in you," said the apostle John, "than he who is in the world" (1 John 4:4 NASB).

OK, Paul, you've made your point. I'll give you this one. Maybe my enemies are no match for God, but what about my needs? And man do I have needs!

"My Needs Are Just Too Many; They Are, Quite Simply, Overwhelming"

Here we confront the second of our three seemingly overwhelming fears: my needs are so many, so deep, and so diverse that I live in constant fear that I'm going to come up short. I need faith that God is going to do what he promised he'd do. I need strength to resist temptation. I need wisdom to navigate some really tough decisions that are ahead of me. I need joy in Jesus to keep me from seeking satisfaction in what the world offers. Boy, do I have needs!

"Yes, I know," says Paul. "But just as your fear of enemies and adversaries led me to ask you a question, so too does your fear that your needs are too many. You're afraid that God either can't or won't provide you with what you need every day to stay true to him. Well, here's my question for you: How will he not also . . . graciously give us all things?" (see Rom. 8:32).

Now again, if Paul had merely asked, "Won't God give us all things?" we might have wondered. We might have said in response, "Well, you know, I need so many things, big things, important things; how can I be certain God will provide them? I'm not saying he lacks the power to do so, but what if he lacks the will?"

But look at how Paul phrased the question. The God who Paul says will graciously give us all things is the God who "did not spare his own Son but gave him up for us all." In other words, the God about whom we ask if he will give us all things that we need is the very God who has already given us his very own beloved Son, Jesus Christ! We encountered this same argument from Paul (see chapter 10) back in Romans 5:9–10: "Since, therefore, we have now been justified by his blood, much more shall we be saved by him from the wrath of God. For if while we were enemies we were reconciled to God by the death of his Son, much more, now that we are reconciled, shall we be saved by his life."

Since God has done the unspeakably and indescribably great and costly thing, namely, sacrifice for us his only begotten Son, we may be fully confident that he will do what is by comparison immeasurably less. Why was God's gift to us of Jesus Christ the greatest imaginable thing for God to do? Because he loves his Son infinitely; his own Son, his dear Son. It wasn't an angel that he sent into this world clothed in flesh to suffer at the hands of evil men and be nailed to a cross. It wasn't one of the four living creatures from the book of Revelation. It wasn't you or your next-door neighbor. It was his precious, only begotten, eternal Son! Further, giving this Son was the greatest thing God could do because his Son did not deserve to die. His Son deserved worship and honor and praise, not spitting and beating and scorn and crucifixion.

The point is this: If God would do the greatest thing for you, he will certainly do all lesser things. You live in fear that God won't do all lesser things and meet all these many needs you have to stay faithful to him. No. In comparison with giving Christ Jesus, it's a breeze! It's a cake walk! Giving you all things is easy. This is the unbreakable, unshakeable logic of heaven.

Let's go back to verse 32. Look at what Paul says. He speaks of something God didn't do and something God did do.

Negatively, God did not "spare" his own Son. Again, let's be clear about who it is that God did not spare—it was his own Son. There is only one Son of God and he is infinitely precious to the Father. Parents, we spare our children when we refrain from inflicting on them all the discipline that their disobedience calls for. Judges spare criminals when they reduce or suspend a sentence. But this is precisely what God did not do with Jesus. He did not withhold one stroke of his holy wrath in punishing Jesus for what we have done. No mitigation, no lessening of the penalty, no suspension of the sentence, no leniency.

Positively, he "gave him up" for us all, or better still, he "delivered" him up. Who delivered up Jesus, and why? Was it Judas Iscariot, and did he do it for thirty pieces of silver? No. Was it the Jewish religious leaders, and did they do it out of jealousy? No. Was it Pontius Pilate, and did he do it out of fear of the crowds? No. It was God the Father, and he did it because of love for you and me. "The wisdom of God," says John Piper, "has ordained a way for the love of God to deliver us from the wrath of God without compromising the justice of God."[2]

Therefore, God will do what is by comparison infinitely easier. He will give us all things that we need for spiritual success. Whatever is necessary for you to make it to the end of life still faithful and still trusting Christ, God will give you. Whatever is necessary for you to be conformed to the image of his Son and to resist temptation, he will give you. By "all things" Paul means everything essential to knowing, loving, adoring, and enjoying him more. Everything you need to find complete satisfaction for your soul and joy for your heart, God will most assuredly supply.

Simply put, God will not withhold anything from you that is essential for your enjoyment of him! Think about what kind of person you would be and the kind of life you would live if you really believed

2 John Piper, *Desiring God: Meditations of a Christian Hedonist* (Colorado Springs: Multnomah Books, 2011), 61.

Romans 8:32. You know that Jesus calls on us to deny ourselves, take up our cross, and follow him daily. You know that he calls on us to lay up for ourselves treasure in heaven and not on earth. You know that he warns us that if we follow him, we will suffer persecution, whether slander or gossip, injustice, mockery, imprisonment, or death. You know that we are called by our Lord to embrace humility and meekness and gentleness and to pursue purity of life.

So why don't we do these things? One of the biggest reasons is fear. We are afraid of being stranded and left to ourselves, trampled on, exploited, and left with nothing. The bottom line is that we are not persuaded that God really will provide us with all that we need to live the life that he's called us to live. Our fear is fueled by unbelief. But Paul puts these fears to rest.

"My Sins Are Simply Too Numerous"

We've come now to the third and final reason why we fear that God's love just won't last, that somehow, someday, in some way or other God will pack up and leave us to ourselves, forever: my sins are too numerous, too many, too great, too serious, too frequent, and the guilt, shame, and feeling of being disqualified are so over-whelming that it doesn't make sense to pretend any longer. Here is Paul's answer. Listen closely to what he says in verses 33–34: "Who shall bring any charge against God's elect? It is God who justifies. Who is to condemn? Christ Jesus is the one who died—more than that, who was raised—who is at the right hand of God, who indeed is interceding for us."

Here, Paul isn't saying that people won't charge us with wrongdoing. They do it all the time! He's not suggesting that Satan won't make every effort to condemn us by bringing up to God and to our own consciences the many ways we have failed.

But all such charges fall short. All such accusations are to no avail. Why? Is it because we are innocent of what our enemies accuse us of? No. In fact, we are probably guilty of a lot more than they can think of or find time to mention! Rather, their accusations are to no avail because "Christ Jesus is the one who died" for us (v. 34). The penalty that those sins call for, whether they be past, present, or future, has already been paid in full. How can anyone condemn you when Christ has already been condemned in your place? What is left for you to suffer? What guilt or penalty remains that might damage your relationship with God?

And it doesn't stop there. Jesus not only died but was raised from the dead to testify to the sufficiency and perfection of what he accomplished for you on the cross. And he not only was raised from the dead but was exalted to the right hand of God the Father, the place of supremacy, power, and honor, in order to demonstrate his power and authority and so that he might "intercede" on your behalf (v. 34). Each time an accusation is brought against you, Jesus turns to the Father and declares, over and over and over again, that he was reckoned guilty for that sin. He died for it. God's justice has been satisfied.

This is the basis or ground on which Paul declares in verse 33, "It is God who justifies!" God is the one who declares that you are righteous in his sight, no matter how loudly your enemies may say that you are guilty, how viciously Satan may attack you, or how painfully your own conscience may scream in protest. It is God who justifies you! Who, then, could possibly bring a charge against you that might stick?

It's one thing for a county court judge to acquit you of a crime. It's one thing for the governor of your state or the US president to pardon you. It is something altogether different and greater when the Judge of the universe declares you forgiven, free, and not guilty. And there is no one, not even you or your sin, who can overturn or reverse his verdict.

When, exactly, did God do this? As we previously read in Romans 5:6, God justifies the "ungodly." God passed a favorable sentence on your behalf in full view of your moral failures, in full view of your shortcomings. God justified you with his eyes wide open! He knew the very worst about you at the time he accepted you for Jesus's sake. God didn't wait until you were "godly" and then justify you on the basis of what you achieved. He looked at you in full and exhaustive awareness of every sin you would ever commit, and because of what Jesus achieved, he declared you righteous in his sight.

Paul knows how easily the conscience of some Christians can become sensitive, self-condemning, and insecure. So Paul here speaks directly

> to the fear that present justification may be no more than provisional, and may one day be lost by reason of the imperfections of one's Christian life. Paul does not for a moment deny that Christians can fail and fall, sometimes grievously. . . . But Paul denies emphatically that any lapses now can endanger our justified status. The reason, he says in effect, is simple: nobody is in a position to get God's verdict reviewed![3]

There are three primary reasons so many Christians live in anxiety and fear about their future with God: too many enemies, too many needs, too many sins. But Paul silences all three!

3   J. I. Packer, *Knowing God* (Downers Grove, IL: InterVarsity Press, 1993), 248.

No Separation, Ever!

For some of you, I suspect that may still not be enough. You still live in fear that God's love won't last. You are still terrified that something somewhere at some time will wrench you from God's loving embrace. That's why Paul writes what he does in verses 35–39:

> Who shall separate us from the love of Christ? Shall tribulation, or distress, or persecution, or famine, or nakedness, or danger, or sword? As it is written,
>
> > "For your sake we are being killed all the day long;
> > we are regarded as sheep to be slaughtered."
>
> No, in all these things we are more than conquerors through him who loved us. For I am sure that neither death nor life, nor angels nor rulers, nor things present nor things to come, nor powers, nor height nor depth, nor anything else in all creation, will be able to separate us from the love of God in Christ Jesus our Lord.

Here again Paul addresses that gnawing fear in your soul that someday, in some way, Jesus will stop loving you: "I've had enough! I'm fed up! I've given you every opportunity, every chance, every benefit of the doubt! It's over! Get out of my sight!" Perhaps you think this way because others who have said they would never cease loving you finally did, and what reason do you have to believe that God is any different from them? So here Paul goes to great lengths to drive home the point. He scans the scope of human adversity to try to find some experience that has the potential to undermine our faith and destroy God's love for us.

Perhaps one day when I'm suffering some trial or persecution, I won't respond the way I should. I'll get angry at God or bitter or curse his name. Maybe *tribulation* (v. 35) will separate me from the love of God in Christ. No.

What about the inner turmoil and *distress* (v. 35), the emotional anxiety, the doubts and fears and despair I so often feel? Will God someday look at my heart and say he's had enough? No.

Will what others can do to me—critical words, rejection, loss of job and income, physical abuse, and other forms of *persecution* (v. 35)—separate me from the love of God in Christ? No.

If I should ever go *hungry* or *without clothing* (v. 35), exposed to untold *danger* (v. 35) and threats or perhaps even killed, decapitated by the *sword* (v. 35), or slaughtered as just so many sheep (v. 36), does that mean God has abandoned me and cut me off from his love in Christ Jesus? Or what if I respond to those challenges with doubt and anger and resentment? Won't that drive God away? No.

It is "in all these things," all of them, every one of them, that "we are more than conquerors" (v. 37). It is "in" them, not by evading them or being spared the devastation they bring, but right smack-dab in the middle of them, we conquer through Christ. Yes, it is "through him who loved us" that the conquering comes. It isn't through our courage, resolve, endurance, or determination that we conquer but through the presence of Christ at all times and on the basis of what he has accomplished. It is not our hold on him but his hold on us that enables us to stand securely through the very worst.

As if to hammer the final nail into the coffin of our doubts and fears, Paul finishes his list of every conceivable threat to the steadfast love of God for us in verses 38–39.

Death can't sever you from his love. In fact, it only serves to bring you into his glorious presence! Nor is there anything that *life* can throw your way that might cut you off from his affection. Paul has in mind not only death itself but the variety of ways in which it might come upon you as well. Thus, neither cancer nor a car wreck, diabetes or drowning, no manner of life's end, whether swiftly by martyrdom or slowly in a nursing home, can put an end to the love God has for you in Jesus. Neither tragedy nor triumph, no manner of success or failure, nothing that we encounter or experience during our earthly sojourn has the power to undermine God's commitment or overthrow his purpose in bringing you safely into his eternal kingdom. Neither good angels nor demonic rulers can cut us off from God's steadfast love. The point is that "there is no spiritual cosmic power, whether benevolent or malevolent, which will be able to separate us from God's love in Christ."[4] Neither the holy angels who do God's bidding nor the demonic rulers who oppose his will have the power to threaten your security in Christ.

Nothing now, in the present, or anything in the future can cut us off from the secure affection of our Father. No supernatural force, no miraculous event, nothing, no matter how strong it may seem, can separate you from Christ. Nothing up there ("height") or down here ("depth") or anything else in all creation can disrupt our union with Christ. The final phrase—"anything else in all creation" (v. 39)—is designed to close off any possible loopholes. No being, no thing, no event, nothing that is or ever will be, not even yourself (after all, you are a created thing) will be able to separate you from the love of Christ!

What about God himself? He's not created. He's the Creator. So maybe he'll separate me from the love of Christ. But the whole

---

4   C. E. B. Cranfield, *A Critical and Exegetical Commentary on the Epistle to the Romans* (London: T&T Clark, 1975), 1:442.

point of Paul's argument in Romans 8 is to reassure you that God is on your side and eternally "for" you (v. 31).

Conclusion

Perhaps you grew up in a home where all you heard were shame-filled words of condemnation. You were constantly reminded of all your failures and sins. You rarely heard affirmations that encouraged and reminded you of God's steadfast love and forgiving grace. Well, if that's you, hear what God says to you through the words of Paul: God is for you! There is no one to condemn you. There is no sin of yours that Christ hasn't already suffered punishment for. Jesus stands at God's right hand interceding and praying for you, every single day. Do you feel the force of this truth? Can you sense the clean air of God's loving power blowing through your heart, elevating you above the self-contempt and self-hatred that has kept you in bondage for so long? That depth of freedom, joy, peace, and healing can be yours right now.

12

Saved by the Love of a Sovereign God

LIKE OUR FEARS ABOUT GOD'S LOVE, the biblical doctrine of election and predestination is frightening to many people. They would rather the subject never be raised and that they would never have to give it a second thought. But the apostle Paul, among other New Testament authors, won't allow it. And they won't allow it because they know that the foundation of God's sovereign choice to save is rooted in his steadfast love. In this chapter, we'll explore God's steadfast love as revealed in the doctrine of divine election.

Foreloved

The word "foreloved" may sound odd to you the first time you hear it. In fact, outside of what the Bible says about divine election, I doubt if it has ever appeared in normal conversation among Christians. But it points to one of the more glorious truths about God's steadfast love, namely, that it existed in the heart of God before the very foundation of the world. Here is how Paul said it in Romans

8:29–30: "For those whom he foreknew he also predestined to be conformed to the image of his Son, in order that he might be the firstborn among many brothers. And those whom he predestined he also called, and those whom he called he also justified, and those whom he justified he also glorified." There is a lot in these two verses that could occupy us for a long time, but my concern is with the reference Paul makes to foreknowledge and predestination and what these words tell us about God's steadfast love.[1]

We all agree that God is omniscient. He knows everything. But "foreknowledge" here in Romans 8:29 cannot refer to God's exhaustive knowledge in advance of the mere existence of all men and women because he clearly says that "those whom he foreknew he also predestined to be conformed to the image of his Son." Unless you are prepared to affirm universalism—the idea that all of humanity will be saved and conformed to the image of Jesus—you must affirm that foreknowledge is not the same as omniscience.

In both Old and New Testaments, the verb "to know" often refers to something far more than mere mental or intellectual understanding. It cannot be restricted to having knowledge in advance of some particular event. Rather, it is used as a virtual synonym for "love." It means to set one's affection on, highly regard, or delight in someone with particular interest.[2]

You may recall the words of Jesus in Matthew 7:23 where he reveals his future response to false disciples at the last judgment: "I never knew you, depart from me." Needless to say, Jesus obviously knew who these men were and what they had done. In fact,

---

1   This chapter has been adapted from my book, *Chosen for Life: The Case for Divine Election* (Wheaton, IL: Crossway, 2007), 103–110. Used by permission.

2   The verb "to foreknow" occurs five times in the New Testament (Acts 26:5; Rom. 8:29; 11:2; 1 Pet. 1:20; 2 Pet. 3:17). The noun "foreknowledge" occurs in two texts (Acts 2:23; 1 Pet. 1:2).

it is precisely his knowledge of their motivation and intentions that leads him to pronounce this word of condemnation. So when Jesus says, "I never knew you," he means "I've never been in a covenantal, saving, intimate relationship with you."[3]

We see much the same thing in Amos 3:2. There the prophet quotes God himself, who says of Israel, "You only have I known of all the families of the earth; therefore I will punish you for all your iniquities." But God obviously knows or has cognitive awareness of all the nations of the earth. He is not ignorant of any of them. Clearly, then, to "know" in this case (as also in Gen. 18:19; Ex. 33:17; Jer. 1:5; Hos. 13:5) is more than just being aware of someone or something. It refers to a knowledge that entails covenant commitment, love, and a relationship of intimacy. Thus, to foreknow is to forelove. We see this in Romans 11:2 where Paul mentions God's eternal, covenant love for Israel, saying "God has not rejected his people whom he foreknew." To have foreknown them is to have foreloved them.

So in Romans 8, Paul isn't merely saying that God thought about you in eternity past but that he loved you before the worlds were formed. That God foreknew us is but another way of saying that he set his gracious and merciful regard on us, that he knew us from eternity past with a sovereign and distinguishing delight. God's foreknowledge is an active, creative work of divine, steadfast love. It is not bare pre-vision or knowing something in advance of it occurring. God's foreknowledge does not merely recognize a difference between people who believe and those who do not believe. Rather, God's foreknowledge creates that difference (see

---

3 See S. M. Baugh, "The Meaning of Foreknowledge," in *The Grace of God, The Bondage of the Will*, ed. Thomas R. Schreiner and Bruce A. Ware (Grand Rapids, MI: Baker, 1995), 183–200.

2 Tim. 1:9; Rev. 13:8; 17:8). No one put it better than Charles Spurgeon. Meditate deeply on his explanation:

> In the very beginning, when this great universe lay in the mind of God, like unborn forests in the acorn cup; long ere the echoes awoke the solitudes; before the mountains were brought forth; and long ere the light flashed through the sky, God loved His chosen creatures. Before there was any created being—when the ether was not fanned by an angel's wing, when space itself had not an existence, where there was nothing save God alone—even then, in that loneliness of Deity, and in that deep quiet and profundity, His bowels moved with love for His chosen. Their names were written on His heart, and then were they dear to His soul. Jesus loved His people before the foundation of the world—even from eternity! and when He called me by His grace, He said to me, "I have loved thee with an everlasting love: therefore with lovingkindness have I drawn thee"[4]

That's right. God's steadfast love has existed from all eternity! It isn't something that arose in the heart of God at some point in centuries past. It was pre-temporal, and it alone accounts for why you are now a believer in Jesus Christ.

Predestined

"Predestination," another term widely misunderstood, is not synonymous with "foreknowledge." Foreknowledge is the distinguishing and steadfast love of God whereby people are elected. Predestination is the decision God made regarding what he intended to do

4 Charles H. Spurgeon, *Autobiography*, vol. 1, *The Early Years, 1834–1859* (Carlisle, PA: Banner of Truth, 1973), 167.

with those he foreknew (see Acts 4:28). Predestination is that act in eternity past in which God ordained or decreed that those he had set his steadfast love on would inherit eternal life. So predestination refers to an action taken by God before the world existed. It points to his eternal, pre-temporal decree of what he would bring to pass in time, in history (see also John 10:14–16, 24–30; Acts 13:44–48; 2 Thess. 2:13).[5] There are six texts in the New Testament where this verb is used, including Acts 4:27–28, 1 Corinthians 2:7, and Ephesians 1:3–6, 11–12. Two of them are here in Romans 8:29–30.

The ultimate purpose of predestination was the establishment of God's spiritual family, his adopted sons and daughters in union with the Son of God, Jesus Christ. God foreknew us and predestined us to become like Jesus—spiritually, morally, and physically. This is what it means "to be conformed" to his "image" (v. 29). Frank Thielman explains, "The term 'firstborn' . . . refers to Christ's status both as the first human being released from bondage to decay (see 1 Cor. 15:20–23) and the first in importance among God's children."[6] Passages like Psalm 89:27 and Colossians 1:15, 18 clearly show that the "firstborn" refers to preeminence of status.

Predestined in Love

Other than Romans 8–9, Paul's comments on predestination in Ephesians 1 are generally regarded as among the more important explanations we have of this doctrine in the New Testament. Let's look at seven truths concerning election that Paul emphasizes. As we make our way through each point, don't lose sight of how each

---

5 This paragraph was first published in Sam Storms, "Foreknowledge—Romans 8:29–30 & 1 Peter 1:1–2," Monergism, https://www.monergism.com/.

6 Frank Thielman, *Romans*, Zondervan Exegetical Commentary on the New Testament (Grand Rapids, MI: Zondervan, 2018), 411.

step is simply the outworking or unfolding of God's steadfast love for his people.

First, as I briefly noted above, election is pretemporal: it was "before the foundation of the world" that God the Father chose us in Christ (see 2 Tim. 1:9–10; 2 Thess. 2:13; see also 1 Thess. 1:4). This shows us that the divine decision concerning human destiny is wholly unaffected by human deeds. To say that God chose us before the existence of all created things is to say that he chose us without regard to any created thing. Election is not something that awaits some event in human history, either the work of Jesus on the cross or the faith of people. It antedates all human history. God's choice is not dependent on human merit or temporal circumstances. Rather, God sovereignly elects us unto eternal life before we exist and without our consent. That isn't to say that our voluntary consent isn't important—we must still believe in Jesus. But our belief is itself the historical and experiential fruit or effect of God's pre-temporal elective decree and steadfast love (see Eph. 2:8).

Second, the objects of divine election are people. Contrary to what some theologians have argued, the object of God's elective choice in Ephesians 1:4 is not Christ but "us" (*hēmas*). In 2 Thessalonians 2:13, Paul declares that "God has chosen you from the beginning for salvation" (see also Acts 13:48). Paul uses the plural "you" in Ephesians for two reasons. First, it would be impossible to use the singular. Second, what is a multitude if not a composite of the many individuals who comprise it? In other words, what is the corporate church if not a collection of individuals to each of whom the blessing comes? Remember that Paul is writing to every person in the church at Ephesus, each of whom is the object of this particular "spiritual blessing" that extends to the entire church. The plural here simply indicates that all believers in Ephesus are chosen by God. It is a blessing common to everyone. That includes us as well.

The third truth Paul emphasizes in this passage is the immediate purpose or goal of election. God chose us so that we might be "holy and blameless" in his glorious presence. Among scholars, these two words have been the cause of considerable debate. On the one hand, some argue that Paul is using these terms to refer to the daily experience of each believer, what we call progressive sanctification (see Titus 2:14; 1 Thess. 4:7; 1 Pet. 1:1–2). No one doubts that the word "holy" is frequently used to describe the character of Christian living, but what about the word "blameless"? It is a word that sounds as if it means "sinless perfection," but in Philippians 2:15, Paul urges believers "to be blameless and innocent, children of God above reproach in the midst of a crooked and perverse generation, among whom you appear as lights in the world" (NASB; see Rev. 14:5). Therefore, it is surely possible that in Ephesians 1:4 Paul is referring to the holiness and blamelessness of the Christian in the here and now of daily life.

Yet, on the other hand, the Greek word translated here as "blameless" is also used in Ephesians 5:27, Colossians 1:22, and Jude 24 to describe the church in its final state of perfection and glory. Further, in these passages we find the notion of being presented blameless "before him," that is, before God. The only other occurrences of this word in the New Testament are in Hebrews 9:14 and 1 Peter 1:19, both of which refer to the blamelessness of Jesus Christ. All this persuades me that Paul is referring to that absolutely sinless, holy, and blameless condition in which we shall be presented to God at the second coming of our Savior. Of course, this by no means excludes the notion of progressive sanctification. Indeed, experiential purity and holiness in this life is a prelude to our ultimate glorification in the next. The latter is the consummation of the former.

On either view, the fact remains that if our personal holiness and blamelessness are the effect or end for which we were chosen, they cannot be the ground or cause of our election. It cannot be the case that God foreknew any degree of holiness or blamelessness in us and on that basis chose us in his Son because we were not holy before he decided to make us holy. It would be absurd for Paul to say, "God chose you to become holy and blameless because he foresaw that you are holy and blameless."

We must not overlook the words "before him" (v. 4). It isn't that the elect are counted righteous in the sight of other men and women but in the sight of God, whose piercing glance sees through all our facades and disguises.

Note also that in verse 5, our election, predestination, and adoption are ascribed to the "good pleasure" of God's "will" (NASB). If God must elect people because he foresees their faith, what would be the point of saying that they are elect according to his "good pleasure"? On any other theological scheme of divine election, God's "good pleasure" is irrelevant. What God "wills" or does "not will" and what "pleases" or "displeases" God would have nothing to do with election. If election is conditional on foreseen faith, it becomes a matter of obligation, duty, and requirement, not good pleasure and sovereign choice (see Matt. 11:26; Luke 10:21).

This also means that election pleases God. He likes it. God didn't predestine us unwillingly, grudgingly, or reluctantly. He wanted to do it. He delighted to do it. God has an emotional life. There is immense and unfathomable complexity in his feelings: He delights in some things, and despises others. He loves and hates. He rejoices and judges. Choosing hell-deserving sinners to spend an eternity with him as his beloved children is uniquely joyful, pleasing, exciting, and satisfying to the heart of God! Should it not also then be a joyful, pleasing, exciting and satisfying truth to our hearts? Should we not, then, talk of it often, sing of it often, and tell it to others often? God's pleasures must become our pleasures. We must learn to rejoice in what he rejoices in.

The fourth important point to be made concerns the relationship between election and being predestined to adoption. What is the connection, if any, between verse 4 and verse 5? Is Paul saying that God elected us because he predestined us to adoption? That is certainly possible, but it's not probable. I believe his point is that God elected us in this way, that is, by predestining us to adoption. Therefore, election, at least in part, consists in being predestined to become a child of God.

One of the more enlightening and encouraging biblical passages on adoption as an expression of God's steadfast love is found in 1 John 3. The concluding verse of 1 John 2 speaks of men and women, like you and me, as having "been born of him" (1 John 2:29), that is, born again or regenerated by the love of the Father through the power of the Spirit. As we move into 1 John 3, we see that the apostle is overwhelmed at the idea that the infinitely righteous God would see fit to beget children who reflect, as a consequence, his righteous character. As you read this passage, take note of the obvious surprise and joy in John's words:

See what kind of love the Father has given to us, that we should be called children of God; and so we are. The reason why the world does not know us is that it did not know him. Beloved, we are God's children now, and what we will be has not yet appeared; but we know that when he appears we shall be like him, because we shall see him as he is. And everyone who thus hopes in him purifies himself as he is pure. (1 John 3:1–3)

Here, the word translated "what kind" (*potapēn*) is perhaps better rendered as "how great" (see the NASB). It originally meant "Of what country?" and suggested surprise and astonishment. John is flabbergasted at such love, and so should we be.

However, this love is not merely shown to us but is "given" to us. The love of God has actually been imparted to or infused in us. It is an aspect of the divine nature that takes up residence in the believer through regeneration. Christians exhibit the love of God not simply because they are imitating an external model but because such love is now an actual component of their inner nature.

This giving of God's love has thus made us his children. The Greek term used here, *tekna*, stresses the community of nature—the nature of God becomes ours through begetting. Not only does God *call* us his children, we actually *are* his children! It is more than a title. It is a reality of status. The title points to the actual reality.

Because of this experience of regeneration, we should not expect the world's recognition. The world did not know Christ and we are partakers of his nature through the new birth, thus the world will not know us. If the world refused to acknowledge the glory and righteousness of our Lord, we in whom he dwells should expect no more.

We return now to Ephesians 1 and the fifth, and perhaps most important, truth that Paul emphasizes—he says that we were chosen "in Christ." Some insist that an individual is chosen for salvation because and only after he puts himself in Christ by an act of free will. In other words, God foreknows that we will fulfill the condition so we are then put "in Christ," and on that basis he elects us. Others insist that it is not individuals who are elect but Christ himself (although, as noted above, Paul does not say here that "Christ" is elect but that "we" are). Thus they insist that it is only because we are in Christ (by free will, of course), who is himself the one true elect person, that we as individuals may be said to be elect ourselves.

It must be admitted that the clause "in Christ" is ambiguous. By itself, it says neither that we are elect because we are in Christ nor that we are elect so that we shall be in Christ. Maybe Paul means that it is "in union with Christ" that we are chosen. I have no problem with that, but the question remains, how did we come to be "in union" with Christ: by free will or by free grace or by some other avenue? Did our union with Christ precede or follow our election? Was it the cause or the consequence of election? Or is our union with Christ simultaneous with our election, perhaps even synonymous with it? In other words, simply saying that God chose us "in union with Christ" does not tell us how or when that "union" came about or whether it has anything to do with the basis for our being chosen. In all likelihood, "in Christ" simply means "through Christ," or, to say it negatively, "not apart from Christ."

In summary, when God in sovereign, steadfast love elected a people from the fallen mass of humanity, he never intended to save them apart from his Son but only by what his Son, the Lord Jesus, would accomplish in his redemptive work. Jesus is therefore the means by which God's electing purpose is put into effect as well as the goal of that election, inasmuch as it is God's purpose through election to sum up all things in Christ (Eph. 1:10).

Paul says much the same thing in 2 Timothy 1:9. There we are told that God saved us and "called us with a holy calling, not according to our works, but according to his own purpose and grace which was granted us in Christ Jesus from all eternity" (NASB). If we are given anything in grace it is by virtue of who Jesus is and what he has done and will do, not by virtue of who we are or what we have done or will do. Therefore, we are elect "in Christ," not "in ourselves." It is because of God's love for his Son and his desire that his Son have a people through whom he might be glorified that God chose us. Therefore, we are chosen "in Christ" in the sense that this Son to whom the Father has given us is he through whom this election to life is made ours in experience. His sinless life, atoning death, and glorious resurrection were the means through which God's electing purpose was put into effect.

Finally, the sixth truth Paul emphasizes in Ephesians 1:4–5 is that God's motive in this pre-temporal decision was love. Many have argued that "in love" should be taken with what precedes in verse 4, thus rendering the passage "holy and blameless before him in love." If so, then "love" is one aspect of the purpose we are chosen for. But if "in love" is taken with what follows in verse 5, it refers to the divine motive for our election. I believe the latter is correct. According to 2:4–5 it was "because of his great love with which he loved us" that we were saved. Those who argue for taking "in love" with what precedes insist that it refers to our loving other believers in this life. But if, as noted above, "holy and blameless" refer not to our present experience but final and perfected standing at the coming of Christ, "love" would more likely refer to God's motive in predestining us. Finally, the emphasis throughout the paragraph is on God's motive, intent, and initiative, not human response.

The ultimate goal of divine election, that is to say, the preeminent reason why God did not give all humanity the just reward of their sin, was so that the glory of his steadfast love and grace might be praised. Election was undertaken to establish a platform on which the glory of God's saving grace might be seen and magnified and adored and praised. Thus we see again here a consistent theme in Scripture: all that God does, he ultimately does to glorify himself and to exalt the beauty of his steadfast love.

13

The Father's Loving Passion for His People

WHAT DOES GOD THINK about when you are on his mind? When God meditates on you in his heart, how does he feel? When God focuses his eye on your soul, what does he see? When God opens his mouth to speak of you, what does he say?[1]

Unless I'm totally deluded, I suspect that many of you would answer those questions the same way Susan did when I asked her: "He thinks badly of me, he feels repelled by me, he sees all my ugliness, and he says, 'Yuk!'"

"Nothing could be further from the truth," I told her. "Notwithstanding what you have been told in the past, notwithstanding what you may feel in the present, Zephaniah 3:17 tells us that when God thinks about you, feels for you, and sees you, he opens his mouth and, with joy inexpressible, he sings!" It took quite a while, and

---

1 This chapter has been adapted from my book *The Singing God* (Lake Mary, FL: Passio, 2013), 1–2, 9–16, 18–19, 21–32. Used by permission.

only with the help of the Holy Spirit, for me to persuade Susan of God's passion for her as his daughter.

God's love for you is so infinitely intense and steadfast that he quite literally sings for joy. His affection is so deep that mere words prove paltry and inadequate. His devotion is so profoundly intimate that he bursts forth in sacred song.

I'm talking about each and every one of you who have come to faith in Christ yet remain convinced that no matter how many times I say it, God surely has someone else in mind. No; if you are a child of God by faith alone in Jesus Christ alone, he has you in mind.

"But Sam, you don't know me. You don't know anything about me. You don't know how ugly I am. You've never been around when I've failed, asked forgiveness, and then failed again, ten seconds later. You don't know how poor of a spouse I've been. You've never seen me blow it with my kids, losing my temper and breaking their spirit."

But I don't need to know you. I only need to know God! The issue here isn't one of who you are or what you've done. It's strictly a matter of the character of God and his determination to love you through the immeasurable sacrifice that he made on your behalf when he sent his only begotten Son to suffer in your place on the cross. Nothing else matters.

But before I draw your attention to Zephaniah 3:17, I want to explore a bit more deeply what it means to say that God is love and what God did to demonstrate his affection decisively for each of us. To do this, look with me at the words of the apostle John in his first epistle.

God Is Love

One of the more enduring and challenging questions we face is simply this: Who is God and what is he like? The answer could come from any number of texts in both Testaments. Some would point to Isaiah 6 and insist that the most fundamental attribute or characteristic of God is his holiness. Others would appeal to texts like Ephesians 2:4–10 where the apostle Paul shines a bright light on the twin truths of God's mercy and grace. Then there are the attributes of omnipotence, omnipresence, and omniscience, all of which are emphasized in Psalm 139 and other similar texts.

But twice in John's first epistle we have the unambiguous declaration that "God is love" (1 John 4:8, 16). This statement is found in a passage that has been referred to as the social test of authentic Christianity. John makes it clear that one who claims to know and love God but continues to hate one's brother is a liar, devoid of the truth and living in darkness. Our responsibility to love one another is traceable to two truths: the nature of God as love (1 John 4:7–8) and the concrete display in history of this love when God sent his Son to be the propitiation for our sins (1 John 4:9–11).

John makes explicitly clear that love proceeds from God. He is its ultimate source: "love is from God" (4:7). But we shouldn't be misled by this statement, as if John is saying no more than that love is something God gives or does or provides. While that is certainly true, John is explaining something else—why love finds its origin in God. It is because "God is love" (4:8, 16). Love is more than God's activity in saving sinners. Of course, we should rejoice in the truth that because God loves us with a steadfast and unshakeable affection we are destined for heaven and not for hell. But God loves us this way because love is his very nature. It is who God is. It is what God is.

This is far and away different from saying "Love is God." After all, there are any number of ways in which people "love" others that are in direct violation of God's commandments. Not all expressions of affection are good, holy, and consistent with God's will and character. But *God's* display of affection for *us* is rooted in his nature. God cannot be anything other than love or act in a way that is inconsistent with it. That should not be taken as a denial that God is also light and spirit and jealous and just, together with any number of other assertions in Scripture about who he is. John is not suggesting that when we say God is love we've said everything about God that can be said. He is love, and he is most certainly a whole lot more, indeed infinitely more. But there is something profoundly foundational in God's being that can only be described with the word "love."

Some in the history of the church have argued that the goal of salvation is deification, the notion that people should become gods or in some way experience a transformation in their essential being such that God's nature is infused into theirs, thereby making it like his. The New Testament rejects this notion, yet it does teach that by the power of the Holy Spirit the virtues and perfections of God's personality should be reflected in how we think, feel, and act. In 1 John 4:7, John says that since true love is only from God, the one who manifests such love shows himself to have been born of God and to be one who truly knows God. This does not mean that anyone who shows love is a child of God irrespective of what they believe about Jesus. The true child of God both believes in Jesus and loves like God loves.

But there is another reason why Christians are obliged to love one another. The first, as just noted, is that God is himself love. First John 4 continues on to explain how God's steadfast love is seen and known to be true: in the cross of Christ (4:9–11). We know God loves us because he delivered up his very own, most beloved and cherished Son to die for us. It wasn't primarily to

provide an example of self-sacrifice, teach or exhort, or to demonstrate authority over the demonic that God sent his Son. It was
so that he might "be the propitiation for our sins" (1 John 4:10).
Our only hope for reconciliation and relationship with God is
if the primary obstacle between us is removed. That obstacle is
unforgiven sin and the wrath of God that it invariably provokes.
When Jesus died, he suffered the penalty our sin demanded and
thus exhausted and absorbed in himself the condemnation we
otherwise deserved. Of all that has been said in this book, this is
the preeminent expression of God's steadfast love for sinners: the
sinless life, penal substitutionary death, and bodily resurrection
of Jesus.

But there is one more facet of God's steadfast love that must be
noted. Not only has God's love been shown in the gift of his Son,
as a result of which we are redeemed, justified, and will ultimately
be glorified, but it is perfected or brought to its appointed consummation when those he died for in turn love one another. Listen
to how John put it: "No one has ever seen God; if we love one
another, God abides in us and his love is perfected in us" (1 John
4:12; see 1 Tim. 1:17; 6:16; Ex. 33:20; John 1:18).

But if "no one has ever seen God," how can he be known? In
John 1:18 the answer is given: "the only God, who is at the Father's
side, he has made him known." Fine, but why does John make
such a theological declaration at this point in his argument? Stott
explains that

> the unseen God, who was once revealed in His Son, *is now
> revealed in His people* if and when they love one another.
> God's love is seen in their love because their love is His love
> imparted to them by His Spirit. . . . The words do not mean

that when we begin to love, God comes to dwell in us, but the reverse. Our love for one another is evidence of God's indwelling presence.[2]

In other words, although God cannot be seen in himself, he *can* be seen in those he abides in! The full height of God's steadfast love for us and the purpose it was manifested for is perfected or achieved only when we love one another. John's point is that the end for which God's love as manifested in Christ was designed is not merely our salvation but our love for one another.

This initially strikes us as odd. Yet that is what John asserts. Here we see once again that God's love has a goal. God does not love us aimlessly. John speaks of God's love being perfected or coming to full expression in us. Look at what he says: "By this is love perfected with us, so that we may have confidence for the day of judgment, because as he [Jesus] is so also are we in this world" (1 John 4:17).

I believe that John is saying the same thing as Paul said in Romans 5:5, where he wrote, "hope does not put us to shame, because God's love has been poured into our hearts through the Holy Spirit who has been given to us." The Father's love for his children reaches its intended goal when it produces in them a feeling of security so powerful that they lose all fear of judgment. When our sense of being loved by God becomes so internally intense that we can only smile at the prospect of judgment day, his passion has fulfilled its purpose.

Someone might think it presumptuous to have lost all fear of judgment. But John clearly says that our confidence is rooted in

2   John R. W. Stott, *The Epistles of John* (Grand Rapids, MI: Eerdmans, 1964), 164.

the fact that the believer is "as he [Jesus] is." What could that possibly mean? In what sense is the Christian "as Jesus is" in the world? John may mean that we are righteous just as Jesus is righteous. By faith in him we are justified, declared righteous in the sight of God, and therefore we look forward to judgment day, confident that there is now no condemnation for those who are in Christ Jesus (see Rom. 8:1). That's possible, but I think the answer lies elsewhere.

Look again at 1 John 4:17. John is saying that our confidence is linked with God's love for us and that in some sense we are as Jesus is. These two pieces of the puzzle are put together in John 17:23, where Jesus affirms that the Father loves the disciples "even as" the Father loved Jesus. This is astounding! Jesus is saying that the Father loves us just like or even as he loves Jesus. Think for a moment of the magnitude of affection God the Father has for God the Son—that's how much God loves you. Therefore, when John says that our confidence is rooted in the fact that we are as Jesus is, he means we are loved by the Father as Jesus is loved by the Father. No wonder all fear is cast out (1 John 4:18)! There is no need to fear him who feels only love for you.

The "fear" of which John speaks is not godly reverence for Jesus but the dread of the criminal who stands guilty in a court of law awaiting a sentence. We no longer fear the punishment of God as Judge because we know and are assured of the pleasure of God as Lord, Lover, and Savior of our souls.

John's point, then, is that he who truly loves God will also love his brother. Indeed, God's love for us reaches its designed goal when it is reproduced in us, that is, when we love one another with the love with which God loves us. That is why an absence of love for the brethren precludes the possibility of love for God (4:19–21).

Why Would God Sing?

The steadfast love that God has for us is not only seen in the gift he gave to us of his Son, by whom we are justified and are being sanctified, but also revealed in the passion in his heart, which is so intense he cannot help but break forth in joyful singing![3] Zephaniah 3:17 tell us that "the Lord your God is in your midst, a mighty one who will save; he will rejoice over you with gladness; he will quiet you by his love; he will exult over you with loud singing."

After careful study of this verse, I've come up with my own paraphrase. It's not a word-for-word translation but an expanded rendering of what I think the original author had in mind:

> The Lord your God is with you all the time. He is a powerful and mighty warrior who saves you and fights on your behalf. When he thinks of you, he exults in festive pleasure and with great delight. At other times, when protests arise in your heart, he quiets you and reassures you of his deep and abiding affection. He celebrates who you are with joyful singing.

However you read this passage, the words are stunning. Its force is unmistakable. If ever there were a Scripture verse worth commit-

---

3 Some have questioned the legitimacy of applying this text to Christians today. They contend that it is addressed to Israel, God's old covenant people. But according to Ephesians 2:11–22 and Galatians 3:16 and 29, believing Gentiles are included among the seed of Abraham, equal heirs with believing Jews of all the promises made to the patriarchs. Some say this text is inapplicable because it refers to the future of God's covenant people. That is true, but the principle of what it tells us concerning the character of God is timeless. God doesn't only begin to love us in this way in the age to come—his love spans eternity past into eternity future. And though it is true that the text speaks of God's people corporately, what is the corporate entity if not a collection of the many individuals who comprise it? What applies to the corporate body applies equally to every person who is a constituent part of it.

ting to memory, this is it. It has rightly been called the John 3:16 of the Old Testament.

Some people resist the urge to sing because it makes them feel vulnerable. It brings to the surface passions that they feel more comfortable keeping tucked away, out of sight. Many are determined at all costs to stay in control. Singing is thus a threat to their resolve to keep a grip on their feelings. There's no denying that there is a vast difference between speaking and singing. It goes beyond the mere fact that some people are embarrassed to sing because they lack a melodious voice. Music has a peculiar power. It infuses words with a dynamic energy that speaking could never achieve.

In other words, singing enables the soul to express deeply felt emotions that mere speaking cannot. Singing channels our spiritual energy in a way that nothing else can. Singing evokes an intensity of mind and spirit. It opens the door to ideas, feelings, and affections that otherwise might have remained forever imprisoned in the depths of one's heart. Singing gives focus and clarity to what words alone might only make fuzzy. It lifts our hearts to new heights of contemplation. It stirs our hope to unprecedented levels of expectancy and delight. Singing sensitizes. It softens the soul to hear God's voice and quickens the will to obey.

I can only speak for myself, but when I'm happy I sing. When my joy increases, it cries for an outlet. So I sing. When I'm touched with a renewed sense of forgiveness, I sing. When God's grace shines yet again on my darkened path, I sing. When I'm lonely and long for the intimacy of God's presence, I sing. When I need respite from the chaos of a world run amok, I sing.

Nothing else can do for me what music does. It bathes otherwise arid ideas in refreshing waters. It empowers my wandering mind to concentrate with energetic intensity. It stirs my heart to tell the

Lord just how much I love him, again and again and again, without the slightest tinge of repetitive boredom.

All well and good, you say. But what's the point? The point is this: God sings too!

Sure, he speaks. He tells us what to do. His voice fills the air. He declares and denounces and proclaims and whispers. But best of all, he sings.

Some may find this hard to swallow. But Adam heard God speak in Eden. Moses quaked at God's voice on Sinai. Jesus and John the Baptist listened as the words echoed across the waters of the Jordan River, "This is my beloved Son, with whom I am well pleased" (Matt. 3:17). And if God can speak, why can't he sing? We know he loves music. More than eighty-five times in the Old Testament alone we are either commanded to sing praises to God or read about someone doing it to his delight.

I wonder what God's voice is like when he breaks forth in song. What do you hear when you envision God singing? John Piper answered that question for himself. He wrote,

> I hear the booming of Niagara Falls mingled with the trickle of a mossy mountain stream. I hear the blast of Mt. St. Helens mingled with a kitten's purr. I hear the power of an East Coast hurricane and the barely audible puff of a night snow in the woods. And I hear the unimaginable roar of the sun, 865,000 miles thick, 1,300,000 times bigger than the earth, and nothing but fire, 1,000,000 degrees centigrade on the cooler surface of the corona. But I hear this unimaginable roar mingled with the tender, warm crackling of logs in the living room on a cozy winter's night.[4]

4 John Piper, *The Pleasures of God: Meditations on God's Delight in Being God* (Sisters, OR: Multnomah, 1991), 187.

Aside from the sound of the singing God, we might wonder what he sings and why. That's easy. He sings of his steadfast love for you. Why? Because he loves you! Here is the crowning jewel of Zephaniah 3:17: that God loves you with such emotional vitality that he exults over you with "loud singing."

"Loud singing" or "joyful singing" is the translation of a Hebrew word that appears on several occasions in the Old Testament. It means a "ringing cry" but should not be thought of as an inarticulate shriek or scream. When the choir of Jehoshaphat belted out a ringing cry, it was the substantive declaration, "Give thanks to the LORD, for his steadfast love endures forever" (2 Chron. 20:21). God's people are exhorted to "tell of his deeds in songs of joy" (Ps. 107:22). This requires articulate utterance (see Pss. 105:43; 126:2; Isa. 12:6; 35:10).

What possibly could stir the mighty God of heaven and earth to sing? Not what but who—you! God's delight is in you. You make him glad. He is overjoyed with you. You, his child, are the apple of his eye, the choicest among ten thousand.

There was a time when I struggled to believe and embrace the truth of God's steadfast love. I worried about my sin and guilt, until I read the prophet's declaration that "the LORD has taken away" his "judgments against" me (Zeph. 3:15). And when I fear that my enemies will do me in, I'm reminded yet again that God is "a mighty one who will save" (Zeph. 3:17). He fights on my behalf and vanquishes all who try to persuade me that I'm far too gone and that his love is at best a dream. Even when God feels distant and remote, Zephaniah assures God's children that "God is in your midst" (Zeph. 3:17). The omnipresent God who fills the universe takes special delight in drawing near to us all when we are drowning in doubt.

Perhaps the greatest threat to feeling God's affection is the lingering shame from our past and even our present sin. But there is good news! God promises to "gather the outcast" and to "change their shame into praise and renown in all the earth" (Zeph. 3:19).

That's what this book has been all about: hearing in your heart the heavenly aria of God's unfathomable love for you. He doesn't just say it. He doesn't just write it. He doesn't just tell others who in turn pass the word on to you. God sings to you lyrics like, "I love you, oh how I love you! My child, I love you with a love that is eternally steadfast!" Now, let's dig a bit more deeply into what the prophet said in this remarkable verse of Scripture.

The Father's Presence

We just noted that God is "in your midst." He is always with you. There is never a moment, even when you have fallen short yet again, that he has abandoned you. Just think of it—he is right there where you are, quite literally every second of every minute of every hour of every day, no matter where that may be or in whatever spiritual condition you may find yourself. That may not get everyone excited, but it certainly energized Zephaniah! His response to God's abiding presence is recorded in verses 14 and 15: "Sing aloud, O daughter of Zion; shout, O Israel! Rejoice and exult with all your heart, O daughter of Jerusalem! The LORD has taken away the judgments against you; he has cleared away your enemies. The King of Israel, the LORD, is in your midst; and you shall never again fear evil."

There's no way to tone down this language. You can't escape the uninhibited exuberance contained in these words. Shout for joy! Shout loudly in triumphant exultation! Rejoice and be glad with all your might! God is with us, so celebrate!

Cast aside all reserve. Forget about what others might think or say. Think about God's presence, his abiding fellowship, and throw caution to the wind! Don't worry about the traditions and formalities of men. Let down your guard for once and be jubilant!

When Zephaniah chose the word translated "shout" in verse 14, he intended to make a point. This word carries the force of a ringing cry that calls for the onslaught of battle (see esp. Num. 10:9; Josh. 6:10; 2 Chron. 13:12, 15). Zephaniah is saying that it's OK to get excited about the presence of God. Fill the air with the piercing cry of exultation. Shout for joy! God is with you.

The Father's Power

But what if this God can't do anything about my problems? What good is his presence if he isn't strong enough to help me face my struggles, especially the lingering doubts I have about whether he truly cares for me?

That's not an invalid question. Here's the answer: The God who is present with you is also a God of unlimited power. He is a mighty warrior, a strong and victorious hero who fights on your behalf. I know it sounds strange, but think about it anyway. God is a soldier. He's dressed for battle, armed and ready. He is your champion, your defender. Isaiah exhorts God's people to sing songs of joyful praise because "the LORD goes out like a mighty man, like a man of war he stirs up his zeal; he cries out, he shouts aloud, he shows himself mighty against his foes" (Isa. 42:13).

The Father's Passion

"That's nice," you say. "God's presence comforts me. His power reassures me. But his passion overwhelms me." You may not be comfortable hearing that God is passionate about his people, but there's simply no way to avoid the force of this text: God exults, delights, rejoices, and sings as the expression of his love.

Some theologians are uncomfortable with speaking of God in this way, as if it suggests he is not impassible. I'm keenly aware of and sensitive to their concerns. They want to emphasize that God is not weak, mutable, or subject to fickle feelings provoked by others. I have to agree with them on that point. But it simply won't do to relegate such texts as Jeremiah 31:20 and Hosea 11:8–9 to figures of speech or anthropopathisms. In the former, God proclaims, "Is Ephraim my dear son? Is he my darling child? For as often as I speak against him, I do remember him still. Therefore my heart yearns for him; I will surely have mercy on him, declares the LORD." In the latter, God cries, "How can I give you up, O Ephraim? How can I hand you over, O Israel? How can I make you like Admah? How can I treat you like Zeboiim? My heart recoils within me; my compassion grows warm and tender. I will not execute my burning anger; I will not again destroy Ephraim."

No one fully understands the nature of God's nature. But I do believe God feels. I do believe that in some sense God has emotions, passions, affections. In particular, he experiences delight, pleasure, and, dare I say, ecstasy, over you and me.

Sherwood Wirt goes so far as to suggest that it was out of joy that God created the universe. Personally, I think he's on to something. When we ask why God created the universe, the Bible replies, "So that he might manifest his glory." But why did God wish to manifest his glory? The answer must be because it pleases him to do so. Yet that is just another way of saying it makes God happy.

Theologians rarely speak of joy as a divine attribute. They probably think it is beneath God's dignity (or theirs). But Wirt contends that "God's nature expresses itself most characteristically and distinctively through joy."[5] It was "for his own pleasure and joy," therefore, that "in the beginning God created the heavens and earth." God was delighted with the work of his hands and thus pronounced it good! What he made pleased him.

If the thought of God experiencing pleasure is a jolt to your religious sensitivities, consider what Jesus said in the parable of the talents: "Enter into the joy of your master" (Matt. 25:21). God is a happy God.[6] The glory of heaven is wrapped up in our participation in the very joy that floods the heart of the Father. Isn't this why Jesus came? His desire is for the joy of his own life to become the joy of ours (John 15:11).

One can only wonder at the depths of divine delight in the soul of the Son of God. And Jesus intends for this very joy to fill up and overflow the hearts of his people (John 17:13). We are first to experience joy in God and the joy that God gives but also the very joy that God himself enjoys. God's joy becomes our joy, and in that God takes joy!

All this is just another way of saying that God is ecstatically happy in his love for his little ones. If you still balk at such talk, return with me to Zephaniah 3:17 and look closely at the three statements in the latter half of the verse.

First of all, God "will rejoice over you with gladness" (Zeph. 3:17). What makes this remarkable is that the same language used in verse 14 to describe our rejoicing over God is here used of God's rejoicing over us. We are exhorted to sing. God, too, rejoices with singing. We are to experience joy. God, too, delights over us with joy. Back and forth, as it were, God and his people take turns enjoying one another.

---

5 Sherwood Eliot Wirt, *Jesus, Man of Joy* (San Bernardino: Here's Life, 1991), 22.
6 See Piper, *Pleasures of God*, 47–76.

All of us know what it's like to get excited over God. We read in Isaiah 61:10, "I will greatly rejoice in the LORD; my soul shall exult in my God." But God gets just as excited over you! He himself says, "I will rejoice in Jerusalem, and be glad in my people" (Isa. 65:19).

Better still, God exults over you with gladness or in festive pleasure or with great delight. How else can I say it? When God thinks about you, his child, his heart explodes in glad celebration. There is divine glee and jubilation beyond words when the Almighty God ponders his own. Such is the depth and height of his steadfast love for them.

If you think I'm just making this up, look at how the terms in Zephaniah 3:17 are used elsewhere and ask yourself if "glad celebration" and "glee" and "jubilation" are too strong. 1 Samuel 18:6 says, "As they were coming home, when David returned from striking down the Philistine, the women came out of all the cities of Israel, singing and dancing, to meet King Saul, with tambourines, with *songs of joy*, and with musical instruments." And 1 Kings 1:40 says, "All the people went up after him, playing on pipes and rejoicing with great joy, so that the earth was split by their noise."

Merriment, elation, hoopla, unbridled glee, raucous mirth. That's how we feel about the grace of God and the God of grace. But that's also how he feels about us!

If you are bothered by what seems to be irreverent rowdiness on the part of God, look closely at what comes next in the text. There are actually two ways of translating this phrase, and both have merit. An early version of the NIV translates it, "He becomes quiet as he reflects on his deep love for you" (Zeph. 3:17). This rendering suggests that God is at one moment moved to loud and jubilant delight over you and, at the next, is reduced to silence as he thinks deeply of his love for you.

If this is the correct rendering, the prophet is describing a love that is so deeply felt, so profound, so perfect, that words are inadequate, indeed, unnecessary. To put it bluntly, God is speechless! The all-wise God, the never-at-a-loss-for-words God, the God with perfect insight into every situation, the God who always speaks correctly and with divine precision, is here moved to utter silence! Such is the impact of his love for you. After the clamorous yet spiritual celebration, it is as if God says, "I love you so much that I can't find words to express it. You so perfectly satisfy my every desire and fulfill my every wish that I long simply to embrace you in my arms and quietly enjoy your presence."

On the other hand, the ESV renders Zephaniah 3:17 as "He will quiet you by his love." This rendering suggests that God takes steps to silence our objections to the declaration that he loves us. We protest the very thought of it, we resist the implications, we deny that anything so grand could be true, and God says to our restless souls things like, "Shh! Be quiet! Calm yourself." In a manner of speaking, he pacifies us. He reduces us to silent and satisfied acceptance of this glorious reality.

Depending on the translation you embrace, God's passionate yearning for you is tumultuous and celebrative, tranquil and calm, or both! One moment a party, the next, silent and placid. Such is God's love for you. O. Palmer Robertson is right when he says, "To consider Almighty God sinking in contemplations of love over a once-wretched human being can hardly be absorbed by the human mind."[7]

If there is at any time silence in heaven, it is eventually shattered. Not with cries of disgust. Not with a burst of anger or stinging

7   O. Palmer Robertson, *The Books of Nahum, Habakkuk, and Zephaniah* (Grand Rapids, MI: Eerdmans, 1990), 340.

criticism born of frustration with your failures, but with singing. That's right. God begins to sing—over *you*.

If it were possible to eavesdrop on solar systems millions of light years away, would we hear anything? Is there sound in space? I believe there is one voice that would indeed be heard, one all-consuming, dominant, deafening, reverberating sound. Even now, in the farthest reaches of infinity, among the trillions and trillions of stars yet unseen by human eyes, echoes forth the passionate voice of the Father, singing about his love for you and me.

Loudly and lively, God shouts with joy over his children. He fills the black holes with the light of his steadfast love and sings the stars to sleep with lullabies about you. It isn't extraterrestrial life-forms that one might hear but the glorious presence of life himself, singing in love for his people. That is the steadfast love that God has for his people. For you.

Conclusion

My wife and I didn't have much of a honeymoon, at least by today's standards. We were married on a Friday night, drove from Tulsa, Oklahoma, to Dallas, Texas, on Saturday, and then returned to our home in Norman, Oklahoma, early on Monday to be on time for work. As short as our time in Dallas proved to be, our love was, and still is, of the highest order.

I recall the words of my employer that Monday: "Well, Sam, the honeymoon's over!" Of course, he was right. As much as Ann and I still love each other today after more than a half century of marriage, it simply isn't possible to sustain the intensity of those first few days, weeks, and months of wedded bliss. It doesn't take long until unforeseen habits, irritations, bulging bellies, the loss of hair, and the onset of wrinkles combine to diminish the affection and romantic intensity of the honeymoon. We can't even revisit the hotel where we stayed in Dallas, as it was long ago torn down and replaced by a parking lot.

But "with God the honeymoon never ends."[8] No matter how old we get or how often we fail, God's steadfast love for us remains at the highest possible level. It was the prophet Isaiah who said that "as the bridegroom rejoices over the bride, so shall your God rejoice over you" (Isa. 62:5). Although it was many years ago, I can still recall the ecstatic feeling of intense love as I watched Ann walk down the aisle to join me and we exchanged our vows. So when people ask me, "Sam, how does God feel about you after these many years as a Christian?" my answer is to describe for them the incredible joy and delight I felt on May 26, 1972, when Ann said, "I do."

---

8 Piper, *Pleasures of God*, 176.

Conclusion

May the Lord Direct Your Heart into the Love of God

MY PURPOSE IN THIS SHORT BOOK was to do more than simply explore the truth of God's steadfast love. Of course, I've done that, and I hope that you are sufficiently persuaded from our digging into Scripture that God's love for you is truly steadfast and unchanging. But there was a second goal I had in mind: enabling you to experience that love in genuinely transforming and sanctifying ways.

Some of you may be quick to respond by saying, "Sam, I got the first part. Yes, God's steadfast love is taught in the Bible in countless ways and, at least in my mind, I understand it and believe it. But I'm struggling to experience it. I just don't feel his love. What's wrong with me?"

Well, there are any number of explanations as to why your inner emotional life is dry and numb. It may be because of the crushing weight of obligations and responsibilities that others have placed on you or that you have placed on yourself. The demands piled on us by work and family and church often feel insurmountable and suffocating, almost to the point that we can't feel anything else. The expectations that well-meaning friends put on us are unrealistic and the burden is simply too much to bear. We feel physically drained, relationally exploited, emotionally exhausted, and spiritually beat up. And the most appealing thought of all is quitting! They call this burnout. And most people face it and feel it at some point in their lives, while a few battle it almost daily.

Directed by God into His Love

So what keeps the Christian going? When you feel yourself drowning in what feels like failure, whether it really is or not, or you are frustrated beyond words with people and life and, dare I say it, even with God, what keeps your head above water? Instead of telling you what people often do to cope under such circumstances, let me point you to what the apostle Paul prays for in 2 Thessalonians 3:5: "May the Lord direct your hearts to the love of God and to the steadfastness of Christ." In the preceding verses (especially 3–4), he has spoken of the inevitable attack of Satan against God's people as well as the importance of faithfully obeying all that God has commanded. It strikes me that Paul's prayer here in verse 5 is, at least to some extent, his answer to the questions, "How am I going to withstand Satan's assault? How am I going to find strength to persevere in obedience to what God has called me to do? How can I find the resolve and spiritual energy to not only believe but be changed by God's love?"

So what is it exactly that Paul prays for? Two things in particular are mentioned and form the heart of his prayer. First, he prays that God would enable you and me to experience the reality of his deep and abiding and passionate affection for us as his children. For me, nothing recharges my spiritual batteries quite like the profoundly personal and experiential assurance that God really does love me. In the final analysis, it doesn't matter that others may fail me or reject me so long as I can live and breathe in the reality of God's love.

Second, Paul also prays that we might experience within our hearts the very power that energized and sustained Jesus himself during the course of his earthly ministry. If anyone had a good excuse to quit, it was Jesus. But he didn't. He remained steadfast and wholly committed to fulfilling the mission his heavenly Father gave him. There was a power, an energy, a resource of some sort that enabled Jesus to endure and persevere in the worst imaginable circumstances, and Paul is saying in no uncertain terms that it is also available to you and me! However, as important as this second point is, our focus will be on the first one.

I'm certainly not suggesting that 2 Thessalonians 3:5 provides us with a comprehensive approach to the problem of not experiencing God's love. But I can say with absolute confidence that few things, if any, will more readily sustain and strengthen you for all God has called you to do than the experiential reality of his steadfast love for you and the presence in you of the very power that kept Jesus faithful to the calling of God on his life. So I want to approach this matter by posing a question, stating some principles, and offering some exhortations. Let's get started.

We begin by addressing the question, What does the "love of God" mean? Some argue that Paul is praying that God would direct or lead us into loving God more. That would be a perfectly legitimate prayer request! Yes, we need to love God more and we need God's help to make it happen. But I don't think that's what Paul has in mind here.

Here's why: the phrase Paul uses here is found often in his writings and always, without exception, refers to God's love for us (see Rom. 5:5, 8; 8:39; 2 Cor. 13:14). Also, our love for God is often weak, fitful, and inconsistent. How could the responsibility of loving God more be the encouragement and strengthening I need when it is one of those very things I feel discouraged for having failed to achieve? In other words, one reason I get spiritually exhausted and frustrated is that I don't love God the way I know I should. Finally, we should probably interpret the love of God in the same way we do the steadfastness of Christ. Since this latter phrase obviously refers to the faithfulness that characterized Christ or that comes from him, the love of God likewise would refer to the love or affection that characterizes God and comes from him as well. Therefore, I'm convinced that what Paul is praying for is that God would act in such a way that we are able to feel, experience, and be refreshed by the love he has for us and to be energized by the spiritual energy and commitment that Jesus himself experienced during his earthly life.

The next thing of importance is that this is a prayer, not an exhortation. This is Paul's petition or request directed to God, not a commandment directed to you. Paul isn't speaking to us but rather to God on our behalf. He doesn't say, "You need to feel God's love and lay hold of Christ's endurance, and it's your responsibility to make it happen!" Rather, he prays, "Lord, please graciously and mercifully take the initiative and lead and direct your children into this reality. Oh God, please act in such a way that they are reinvigorated and renewed with a sense of your delight in them and infuse into their souls the power that sustained Jesus."

Note also that Paul is asking that God would act directly upon our "hearts" (see Rom. 5:5). The "heart" here and in most places in Scripture is an all-inclusive term that refers not only to how we think but how we feel. We often read in Scripture of our "inner man" or "inner being" (see 2 Cor. 4:16; Eph. 3:16); this refers to the center or core of our personality. It includes our affections, our wills, and our spiritual senses, so to speak. What this means, then, is that God can, often does, and indeed must exert a powerful influence on our emotional life (see 1 Chron. 29:17–19; Prov. 21:1; Ezra 1:1, 5; Dan. 1:9; 2 Cor. 8:16–17). So "heart" here refers not only to our thoughts and intentions but also to our affections and feelings and choices.

We must also look closely at Paul's choice of terms here, especially his use of the Greek word translated "direct." He has already used this word in 1 Thessalonians 3:11. There he writes, "May our God and Father himself, and our Lord Jesus, direct our way to you." Paul's prayer is that God would remove all the obstacles and hindrances that keep him from making his way to Thessalonica. There are barriers that stand in the way. There are enemies who oppose us, says Paul. There are hurdles that we have to overcome, and we need God's help to make it happen.

What this means for you and me is that there are probably numerous obstacles or stumbling blocks that stand in the way of our feeling the affection of God for us. Entering into the fullness of what it means to know God's steadfast love for us is no easy thing. It certainly doesn't come naturally to us. So let's consider some of the biggest obstacles that hinder us from feeling the depths of God's love.

One of the more powerful lies that makes this a challenge is the false belief that God's affection for me is held hostage by my past. In other words, we live in fear that our past failures govern our present identity and our future hopes. I am what I've done in the past. I am the sins I've already committed. I am what others have done to me. I am what others have said about me. And if that is what I am then it is obvious that God couldn't possibly love me.

We must constantly remind ourselves that our history is not our identity (see 2 Cor. 5:17).

Then there is the false belief that my current circumstances are indicative of God's affection for me. We measure God's love by how successful we are in terms of money, popularity, health, prospects for the future, friends, family, and how we are doing in comparison to others. This false belief is rooted in the assumption that hardship and adversity are signs of God's displeasure and his disappointment with us.

We must also push back against the false belief that God's love for us is based on what we do rather than what Christ has done. We rehearse in our minds all the things we have done or failed to do and then conclude that the strength and steadfastness of God's love is somehow tied to our performance rather than resting in the performance of Christ on our behalf.

An especially troublesome obstacle is the belief that God's knowledge of us will forever preclude the possibility that he will enjoy us or delight in us. We know ourselves all too well. We know our sins, selfishness, weaknesses, failures, and tendency to repeat the same mistakes over and over again. And we despise ourselves for it. We live in self-contempt and self-condemnation. The guilt and shame are at times overwhelming. But if God knows us better than we know ourselves, then he must be a thousand times more disgusted with us than we are with ourselves.

This is when I remind myself of Psalm 103:14. You are probably familiar with all the glorious things God does for us as described in verses 1–13 of this psalm—give us mercy, grace, patience, and steadfast love. It is precisely at this point that my soul so often pushes back against God's word: "But God, how can any of this be true given that you know me infinitely more accurately than I know myself? Surely, your knowledge of how I'm made and what I do will undermine any hope of my experiencing your steadfast love."

That is when the next verse in the psalm comes to the rescue. Immediately after this beautiful list describing God's love and mercy and forgiveness, the psalmist declares, "For he knows our frame; he remembers that we are dust" (v. 14). Hold on. That doesn't make any sense whatsoever. As best I can tell, it is precisely because God knows my "frame" and remembers that I am a descendant of Adam, made from the dust of the ground, that he would never do for me the things that he says he will do in verses 1–13. I think God would reply something to the effect of "Ah, Sam, that's how you think. That's not how I think. Divine logic is immeasurably greater and more persuasive than human logic. It is indeed because ("for," v. 14) I know your tendencies, your bad habits, your disposition, your sinful and selfish ways, that I have graciously chosen to do the very things you think are impossible." Simply put, we must never let our knowledge of God's knowledge of us prevent us from understanding and enjoying his great love for us.

In addition to the many reasons thus far, there are the lies and slander of Satan that daily hammer us in an effort to convince us that a holy God could never love or care about unholy people like us. You know his tactics: "God is embarrassed by you. He's fed up with you. His patience for you has run out. He's done. It's over. You are a pathetic failure. You're hopeless. You're an unsightly wart on the body of Christ. You're too ugly, dumb, sinful, overweight, slow, poor, weak, and untalented, and it's just too darn late." And I'm only scratching the surface of all the many reasons we are convinced God's love for us is a ruse. No wonder Paul felt it so necessary to pray that God would step into the situation and remove the boulders from the pathway to intimacy with him.

But there is one final obstacle to overcome. It is the misguided conviction that God will only love some future version of myself, the me that will one day emerge after my house is in order, my checkbook is in balance, and my bad habits are broken. You should know by now, after reading this book, that God loves the present version of yourself. That doesn't mean he's perfectly pleased with everything in our lives today. But it does mean that our current failures are no barrier to his steadfast love. His love is of such a nature that it finds us where we are and then refuses to leave us there.

Now, back to yet another observation about Paul's language in this single verse. It concerns the primary focus of this entire book: the reality of the love of God for you and me. Having dealt with victims of virtually every imaginable form of abuse and sin, both rich and poor, both well-known and anonymous, I've discovered that the only thing that supplies our souls with lasting hope, promise, encouragement, and energy for tomorrow is the experiential reality of God's steadfast love for us! I'm not talking merely about knowing it to be a fact, knowing it to be a theological truth. This is more than a spectacle to observe, a topic to discuss, or an argument to defend. Don't approach the reality of God's love for you like you would a painting in a museum, such as the *Mona Lisa* in the Louvre, encased behind bulletproof glass and roped off at a distance with security guards surrounding you.

God wants you to feel it. God wants you to be captivated in body, soul, and spirit, to be overwhelmed in the depth of your affections with a tangible sense of his passion and presence. This is what we saw earlier in Romans 5:5, 8:15–17, and especially Ephesians 3:14–21. I don't want to make more of Paul's choice of language than I should, but the preposition he uses (*eis*) should probably be rendered "into" rather than "to." It isn't so much that the Lord is being asked to lead us to his love, like a thirsty deer being led to a refreshing oasis. Rather, we need to be led *into* that love, immersed in it, surrounded by it, engulfed within it. This is why the prayer is that God would exert his power on our "hearts" and not just our minds.

One final observation is in order. Although it is God who must act to make this a reality in our lives, he employs means. He sets before us a pathway to walk along where we are far more likely to encounter him in a life-changing way. The question then becomes, What should I do if I don't feel his love?

Keep Yourselves in the Love of God

To answer this question, we should begin with the exhortation in Jude 20–21: "But you, beloved, building yourselves up in your most holy faith and praying in the Holy Spirit, keep yourselves in the love of God, waiting for the mercy of our Lord Jesus Christ that leads to eternal life." While Paul emphasizes God's initiative in directing us into his love in 2 Thessalonians 3:5, Jude focuses on our responsibility to "keep" ourselves in it.

Yet, Jude is not saying that we should work hard to make ourselves loveable or that we should strive to win God's affection. Earlier in this short epistle, he made it quite clear that his readers (and you and me, by application) are already "beloved" (the Greek is a perfect passive participle of the verb *agapaō).* In verse 21 we are exhorted to keep ourselves in the "love" of God, where "love" is simply the noun form, *agapē.* We are also "kept for Jesus Christ" (Jude 1). Later, in verse 24, Jude will celebrate God's love for his children by speaking of him as the one "who is able to keep you from stumbling and to present you blameless before the presence of his glory with great joy." Although the verb in verse 24 is different from that in verses 1 and 21, the force is the same: God is the one who keeps, guards, and preserves us for salvation.

What this tells us is that since we are the objects of God's steadfast love and affection (his "beloved," v. 1), since we are being "kept for Jesus Christ" (v. 1), and since he is able to "keep" (v. 24) or guard and preserve us from stumbling, verse 21 cannot mean that if we don't do something to "keep" ourselves in his love, we will ultimately be cut off and perish. So, what, then, does verse 21 mean?

The first thing to note is that Jude tells us the way that we are to keep ourselves in God's love. It is by building ourselves up in our most holy faith, praying in the Holy Spirit, and waiting patiently and expectantly for the mercy of Christ that will come to us when he returns. So, yes, there are things we are responsible to do to "keep" ourselves in God's steadfast love. And what Jude means by this is that we are to labor in God's grace, in accordance with what is commanded in this paragraph and elsewhere in Scripture, in order to maintain that spiritual intimacy with God so that we can experience and enjoy the fullness of what it means to be his beloved children (see John 15:9–10).

We don't keep ourselves in such a way that we might gain or win God's affection. Nor do we keep ourselves lest we fall out of favor with him and incur his eternal judgment. We keep ourselves in his love in the sense that we abide in Christ and his word so that we might enjoy what is ours wholly by grace through faith. It is the difference between what I have elsewhere described as our eternal union with God and our experiential communion with him.[1] The former is settled and sealed by his saving grace. It is always and eternally true that we are in covenant union with our God and

---

1 See my book *A Dozen Things God Did With Your Sin (and Three Things He'll Never Do)* (Wheaton, IL: Crossway, 2022), 19–24.

nothing can undermine this (see Rom. 8:31–39). But our experiential communion with him can be disrupted by unconfessed and unrepentant sin. Our capacity to enjoy our eternal union, our ability to experience the peace, satisfaction, and delight that comes from being united with our great triune God, is dependent on our continual trust in his grace and the power of the indwelling Holy Spirit.

Thomas R. Schreiner and Ardel B. Caneday contend that the exhortation in Jude 21 is another way of saying, " 'Do not commit apostasy.' We are to maintain our allegiance to God until the end and not stray from his love."[2] Perhaps. But I think Jude is simply exhorting us to strive in the power of the Spirit to remove every obstacle that hinders us from feeling the presence of God's affection and basking in the liberating light of his saving grace. If I may, then, put 2 Thessalonians 3:5 and Jude 21 together, I think what we are being told is this: You are God's beloved child. But the opportunity for you to experience this steadfast love in the present is dependent on God working in your life to direct you into the enjoyment of his delight in you. Pray that God would overcome whatever fear, hesitation, or anxiety there is in your heart that prevents you from believing that his steadfast love is a reality. And avail yourself of every means he has provided so that you may enter into his love and live peaceably and joyfully in all that it means to be beloved of the Most High.

There are, then, several things we should devote ourselves to as a way to keep ourselves in a posture of mind and heart where the love God has for us can do its work. First, we must daily read God's written word and remind ourselves of its truths. Meditate on

---

2 Thomas R. Schreiner and Ardel B. Caneday, *The Race Set Before Us: A Biblical Theology of Perseverance and Assurance* (Downers Grove, IL: InterVarsity, 2001), 257.

its promises. Reflect on its portrait of God, Christ, and the Spirit. Believe its truths. Trust in its power. And as you read, remind yourself of God's love as demonstrated in the cross. Reaffirm what you know to be true. Defy feelings, or lack thereof, that contradict these truths, and cling in faith to Zephaniah 3:17. Practice not forgetting God's benefits and blessings (Ps. 103:1–3). Stop listening to your irrational and negative thoughts and instead preach the gospel to yourself. The psalmist often scolds himself and argues with his own soul, taking issue with what he feels when it contradicts what he knows to be true. We must learn to talk to ourselves (rather than listen to ourselves): "Self, soul, listen up. God loves you! Look at the cross. Remember the Table of the Lord. Look to the elements of bread and wine. What do they mean? To what do they point?" Remind yourself of the past and look to the future.

Second, "abide" in his love by keeping his "commandments" (John 15:9, 10). "If you keep my commandments," said Jesus, "you will abide in my love, just as I have kept my Father's commandments and abide in his love" (John 15:9–10). Sin numbs the soul, deadens the heart, and renders the spirit deaf and senseless. But obeying Christ allows us to experience his love.

Third, pray. Ask God to renew your affections and increase your capacity to feel his love. Cry out to him often to restore the joy of your salvation, to pour out afresh the Holy Spirit in order to awaken in you a renewed sense of his delight in you. There is no better prayer to launch your day with than that of Psalm 90:14: "Satisfy us in the morning with your steadfast love, that we may rejoice and be glad all our days."

Fourth, worship. Worship your way into the experience of God's love. Permeate the atmosphere in your home, car, and office with songs of praise. Often we must sing *to* joy rather than merely *from* it.

As we saw in chapter 13, God has ordained music as a means of grace whereby truths that our hearts cannot fully absorb through spoken or written words are more easily believed and received.

Finally, never lose sight of the assurance that Jeremiah provides in Lamentations 3: "The steadfast love of the LORD never ceases; his mercies never come to an end; they are new every morning; great is your faithfulness" (3:22–23). This book is now at an end, soon this day will come to an end, and even your life on this earth. But God's steadfast love never will.

General Index

Scripture Index

Also Available from Sam Storms

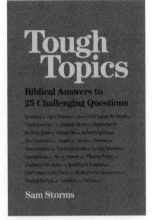

For more information, visit **crossway.org**.